Adult Literacy/Illiteracy in the United States

CONTEMPORARY WORLD ISSUES

Adult Literacy/ Illiteracy in the United States

A Handbook for Reference and Research

Marie Costa
Introduction by Paul V. Delker

89-021

ABC-CLIO

Santa Barbara, California
Oxford, England

Library of Congress Cataloging-in-Publication Data
Costa, Marie, 1951–
  Adult literacy/illiteracy in the United States : a handbook for reference and research / Marie Costa.
      p.   cm.—(Contemporary world issues series)
  Bibliography: p.
  Includes index.
  ISBN 0–87436–492–2 (alk. paper)
    1. Literacy—United States—Handbooks, manuals, etc.
  2. Literacy–United States—Societies, etc—Directories.   I. Title.
  II. Series.
  LC151.C64 1988
  374′.012—dc19   87-31696
  ISBN 0–87436–492–2 (alk. paper)   CIP

10 9 8 7 6 5 4 3 2 1

ABC-Clio, Inc.
Riviera Campus
2040 Alameda Padre Serra
Santa Barbara, California 93103

Clio Press Ltd.
55 St. Thomas' Street
Oxford, OX1 1JG, England

This book is printed on acid-free paper ∞.
Manufactured in the United States of America

This book is dedicated to writers, readers, teachers, and librarians everywhere

Contents

Preface

IN AN AGE OF SOMETIMES frightening complexity, it is a natural—but dangerous—tendency to want to simplify problems and issues, in the hopes of finding simple, quick answers. Although such oversimplification can bestow a temporary feeling of control, power, or accomplishment, too many problems defy simple solutions, emerging more complex and difficult than ever. Further, even though we are living in what has been called the information age, and are surrounded by an abundance of information, our access to that information is often limited. And without usable information, without the ability to know what has been thought, and explored, and dreamed, and tried—successfully and unsuccessfully—we are doomed to be trapped forever in a cycle not only of oversimplification, but of constant reinvention and repetition, of variations on a theme rather than progress.

Like so many other issues of our time, that of literacy has fallen prey to oversimplification and to dramatic resolutions that are doomed to failure because they do not address the real problem—do not, indeed, begin to understand what that problem is. Our inability to resolve the issues of literacy and illiteracy does not stem from a lack of intelligence, or of good intentions, or of enthusiasm. It does not even stem from a lack of money, although more money is certainly needed. Americans are notoriously generous with their time, energy, and money when they have found a cause. Some alarming statistics, along with a heart-wrenching made-for-TV movie or two, and we are called to action, any action, certain that if we are enthusiastic enough, work hard enough, spend enough, and mobilize enough people, we can fix anything. The problem is that, all too often, we don't understand what we are fixing, much less how to fix it.

This book is an attempt to provide a tool, not for "fixing" illiteracy, but for learning about literacy and its role in our lives and our society. It does not provide quick, easy answers; instead it lays a foundation for understanding, and then identifies a variety of resources that can lead to greater understanding, in the hope that understanding will lead in turn to *effective* action. It places current statistics and literacy education efforts in a historical context, sheds some light on the sources of the "alarming statistics," identifies some key players and important resources—both organizations and individuals—and points the way to sources of further information, sources that represent a wide variety of viewpoints and approaches. It is meant for teachers, students, writers, researchers, volunteers, and anyone who is concerned about literacy on an individual or a societal basis, or both. I sincerely hope that it will prove a stimulus for thought, discussion, and further research, that it will lead to more questions and thus to real solutions.

I do not want to imagine the possibility of a society without the breadth, depth, and wondrous variety of knowledge, thought, opinion, wisdom, and sheer beauty that can be imparted through words on paper. Certainly we have the ability to communicate without reading and writing, and I suspect that it is all too possible for society and its members to find ways to function without the printed word. But *function* is not the same as *thrive* or *grow*. We need not only the functionality but the richness and variety of a fully literate society. This book is a small but I hope not insignificant contribution toward building a literate and vital United States, now and for centuries to come.

Acknowledgments

THIS BOOK IS THE RESULT of nearly a year of research, of numerous letters and conversations exchanged with individuals around the country—people who are in the trenches, so to speak, working to understand, to explain, to teach, to encourage literacy. I am deeply grateful to everyone who helped me by giving time, information, and advice. In particular I wish to thank Jim Parker, Elaine Laugharn, and Patricia Lane of the Adult Education Division of the U.S. Department of Education, for their generous supplying of information, contacts, and insight; Peter Waite, Elaine Shelton, and Judy Koloski, who reviewed portions of the book for accuracy and completeness; my editor, Heather Cameron, for her helpful advice and her encouragement when I felt overwhelmed; and, always, my family, for their patience, support, and understanding.

Introduction
Paul V. Delker

THE CONDITION OF ILLITERACY has existed in the United States since its beginning. Among our ancestors, those who could work with the printed and written word were the exception, not the rule. And for most earlier Americans, the absence of literacy skills was not a serious problem: Frontier literacy was more important for those who opened the wilderness, farming literacy for those who provided the nation's food, and social literacy for those who formed and inhabited the new communities. As business and commerce grew, the demand for literacy increased for those who sought to make their living that way, but more than 200 years would transpire before we as a nation would consider the *condition* of illiteracy as the *problem* of illiteracy.

Thomas Jefferson saw a literate and educated populace as a cornerstone of democracy. In the nineteenth century, our nation became committed to universal free education, which included the notion that, in time, every citizen would be literate and comfortable with the printed and written word as part of the fabric of everyday life and learning. That policy appeared to work well with a few exceptions: for example when, because of a lack of literacy skills, some citizens were excluded from voting and others were found unqualified to serve in the armed forces during our world wars. But wars would end, literacy laws would eventually be struck down by the courts, and the condition of illiteracy would not become a national concern.

On 7 September 1983, an Adult Literacy Initiative was launched under the leadership of Secretary of Education Terrel

H. Bell. Proclaiming adult illiteracy as a national problem, the initiative put out a call to action directed especially to the private and voluntary sectors. The response to the call was slow at first, but commitments from private sources and the media generated a national movement whereby the long-standing condition of illiteracy would command the energy and concern characteristic of the attention given a national problem.

Why is it that for the first time in our history we are regarding adult illiteracy as a national problem? Have other generations simply been less aware of its importance, or has the importance of literacy increased? Both are the case. Thomas Jefferson was right in his view of the importance of a literate and educated populace to a self-governing society, and that importance has not changed. But our understanding of the importance of literacy now extends beyond participation as democratic citizens into areas of economic, parental, and social competence. Literacy among those in the workplace is increasingly related to our ability to compete in a world economy. The relationship between family literacy and performance in school is increasingly verified. Functioning freely and effectively as consumers, neighbors, and community members increasingly calls for a significant degree of literacy. The levels of all these requirements and our awareness of the importance of being literate have both increased.

Yet, it may very well be that the most important aspect of literacy—the importance of literacy in personal and human development—is not fully plumbed in all these considerations. The illiterate is today able to get a great deal of information without resorting to the printed word. The amount of information available to a total illiterate today far exceeds what was available to Thomas Jefferson and his peers 200 years ago. But it is impossible to believe that a group of illiterate Americans today could develop a constitution incorporating the wisdom of our Bill of Rights. Illiterates must rely on others for information, and they are limited in their ability to reflect on that information and discern that which is valid. True literacy makes possible inquiry in any direction, in any breadth and depth, and allows a person to access and reflect on past and current wisdom. These are the true qualities Thomas Jefferson supported in his insistence on the importance of a literate and educated populace.

Illiteracy can be viewed from two perspectives: that of society and that of the individual. Both are valid, but they are not the same. Society will view it in terms of economic and social consequences, of the numbers of people unable to function, and the costs incurred and benefits lost. Individuals may view their illiteracy from a variety of perspectives. Some will be aware of it and wish or even seek to become literate. Others, if they count it as a deficiency, may not regard it as important in relation to more immediate and more severe problems. And there are others who do not even regard it as a deficiency and who have never experienced the rewards of literacy either in increasing the ability to function or in exciting the life of the mind and spirit.

Thomas Sticht pointed out in his introduction to the National Adult Literacy Conference held in January 1985 in Washington, DC, that the problem is not illiteracy but literacy. Illiteracy is the absence of literacy. It is the natural state into which we are all born. Thus, the problem is how to impart literacy, not how to eliminate illiteracy. This is a much more profound observation than may first appear. To approach a person in the mode of imparting literacy is to regard that person as a learner. Here is someone who lacks literacy but who can become literate. To approach that same person as an illiterate may imply that the person cannot learn, or is inferior in some way as a human being. It may imply past failures on the part of that person, when that may or may not be true, and be devoid of any critical reflection on what might have caused those failures.

When an adult acquires or extends his or her literacy, that act is a form of adult learning. Until recently, we have associated adult learning with adult education, i.e., the act of learning through a course, seminar, workshop, or similar setting prepared and controlled by an educator or trainer. But we now understand that a real distinction can be drawn between adult education and adult learning. The latter includes any purposeful and deliberate learning whether it occurs under institutional sponsorship or is initiated and controlled by the individual learner. Research conducted over the past two decades discloses that most adult learning is initiated, designed, and conducted by individual adults, is not for credit, and does not depend on those formally trained as educators or trainers.[1] Adults in the United States learn throughout their lives, and they do most of their deliberate and personal learning on their own.

This same research discloses that adults with low literacy

rates and even adult illiterates organize and conduct their own learning projects with almost the same duration and frequency as educated adults. In doing so, they make little or no use of printed resources, but they succeed in setting learning goals and in achieving them. They are among the lifelong learners in our society.

Our research is not extensive enough to tell us to what extent all illiterates are true lifelong learners, but the phenomenon has been consistently confirmed in the experience of adult basic educators over the past 20 years. It seems clear both from what we know about the illiterate's ability to conduct his or her learning and from the point of view of good adult pedagogy that every adult illiterate is and should be approached as a true adult learner. What literacy does for that person is to open new learning opportunities and new resources that would never be possible without literacy skills.

As the requirements for literacy have increased so has the complexity of what we have come to mean by literacy. Early definitions of literacy referred only to the ability to deal with the printed or written word, and the level of material to be mastered was at one time as minimal as reading and writing one's name. Because of the diversity and complexity of today's literacy tasks, the 1986 report of the National Assessment of Education Progress, titled *Literacy: Profiles of America's Young Adults,* rejected any single standard for literacy. To measure modern literacy requirements, the researchers found it necessary to use three scales: a prose scale to measure levels of complexity encountered in reading and interpreting prose as found in newspaper articles, magazines, and books; a document scale for measuring the type of information located in forms, tables, charts, and indexes; and a quantitative scale applying numerical operations to information contained in material such as menus, checkbooks, and advertisements. Thus, when today we speak of teaching someone to read, we include a range of information-processing skills far beyond that formerly associated with the ability to decode simple words and sentences. This complexity of requirements led David Harman to observe that illiteracy exists wherever there are people whose reading and writing skills are inadequate for the situation in which they find themselves.[2] In this latter sense, everyone is to some extent illiterate, a phenomenon that is often confirmed when we ask, What does that mean?

The sophisticated measurement of modern literacy requirements brings the meaning of literacy much closer to our traditional notion of education than to the historical meaning of literacy as the ability to read simple text. For this reason, the phrases "functional literacy" and "basic skills" are preferred by many in an attempt to denote the different reality. Whatever terms one prefers, it is paramount to understand that we are talking about higher requirements of skill and background knowledge than those of even two or three decades ago. This also means that comparisons between our level of literacy today and at some former time are not really meaningful. Comparisons of literacy rates among nations of the world have probably even less significance since these comparisons require adopting absolute standards that abstract from the cultural context in which adults actually function and learn.

By far the most significant knowledge and experience gained in this country about adult literacy has occurred in programs offering basic education for adults rather than in programs designed to teach only reading to adults. In 1965, federal support for adult basic education became available and was later extended to support adult high school equivalency programs. Today, these programs provide educational opportunities for over three million adults annually. They include extensive programs in English as a second language to serve adults who are learning English for the first time. Every state has a network of local programs and state personnel experienced in adult basic education practices and materials. And the resources of the two national voluntary literacy organizations—Laubach Literacy Action and Literacy Volunteers of America—stand ready to provide training and assistance to organizations and groups throughout the cities, towns, and rural areas of our country.

In the United States, business and industry spend more on education and training than local, state, and federal governments combined, but almost all these resources are directed to managerial and professional employees.[3] White-collar workers receive three-quarters of the formal training provided though they represent only one-half of the work force. As a group, professional and technical personnel lead in education and training benefits, receiving twice their share. In contrast, workers with less than a high school education represent about 23 percent of the work force but make up only 5 percent of company trainees.[4]

These figures reflect an assumption that has dominated the U.S. workplace: that a significant portion of jobs in the United States do not require meaningful levels of literacy or basic skills. While that assumption may have been defensible 50 years ago, it certainly is not the pattern of today's workplace. In a 1980 study 70 percent of the reading material found in a cross-section of jobs was between ninth- and twelfth-grade difficulty, and 15 percent was even higher. In military jobs, materials used averaged tenth to twelfth grade in level of difficulty.[5] During the past quarter-century, while managerial, professional, and technical employees have been generously trained and educated, blue-collar employees have been neglected. As a result we now have a serious mismatch between today's jobs and up to one-fifth of our work force. In recent displaced worker projects, up to 20 percent of participants tested showed basic educational deficiencies, and among employed workers the figure may be as high as 15 percent.[6]

Increased awareness of a problem always precedes the allocation of resources to deal with that problem. Under the leadership of Harold W. McGraw, Jr., the Business Council for Effective Literacy is rapidly raising awareness of the significance of the literacy problem in our work force and our communities. During the next five to ten years, we can expect to see business and industry direct new resources or allocate a significantly higher percent of training and education dollars to improving the literacy and basic skills of our work force. This must happen if we are to maintain our position in the world economy.

There are citizens who recognize the value of literacy and are motivated to acquire it as individuals. In most instances, these are the persons on-going programs and voluntary efforts find it easiest to serve. Many others are interested in learning but do not see literacy as directly relevant to what they want to learn. These persons are sometimes termed the hard to reach, but this more accurately describes the perspectives of the educator and the volunteer than that of the learner. If these learners are hard to reach, it is because the content of what they want to learn is not literacy itself. Programs that help them realize objectives they set themselves, conducted at times and places of their preference, may not always bear the mark and appearance of teaching literacy skills, but they have proven to be effective. As their learning progresses, initial goals are replaced with others, and their literacy increases. Often, becoming literate is not their objective, but they become more literate as a means to achieving their objective.

No simple problem merits the full attention and energy of a country as resourceful as ours, but literacy is not a simple problem. Providing opportunities for all citizens to acquire or extend their basic skills is complex and calls for a highly pluralistic approach. There is no "quick fix." If there were, we could continue to be comfortable with the condition of illiteracy and devote our resources elsewhere. As with other problems that have merited our full attention and effort, this one will not be readily resolved.

We know something about how to address the literacy problem, but much more needs to be known, and we are devoting virtually none of our research effort to finding new solutions. Individual and community action, private sector commitments, and voluntary and community-based organizations can do much to solve this problem, but the effort is too important to go forward unaided by research and experimentation. If resources are not forthcoming soon, we as citizens will have to insist that our nation put its money where its mouth is—and where it happily belongs.

Elevating adult illiteracy from *condition* to *problem* acknowledges both the importance and complexity of our becoming a fully literate society. The call to action recognizes that a nation of literates is a nation of learners and that we must apply a major portion of our energies and resources to make that a reality. The voluntary and private sector response embodies a commitment and seriousness equal to the enormity and complexity of the task. As we go forward, we will discover new remedies and new solutions, but we must take care to begin by building on what we already know. That is one of the reasons a sourcebook on adult illiteracy is important.

What we know about adult literacy happily cannot be condensed into one book. Much of what we know is not yet in print but resides in the experience and collective effort of individuals and organizations. They must be accessed as we move adult literacy from the concern of adult educators to the business of all citizens. Those with knowledge and experience can only lead the way if they are known and called upon to share what they know. This sourcebook is designed to help us in that task and in addressing the problem of literacy.

Notes

1. See especially Allan Tough, *The Adult's Learning Projects* (Toronto and Ontario: The Ontario Institute for Studies in Education, 1979), 171–178.

2. David Harman, *Illiteracy: A National Dilemma* (New York: Cambridge, 1987), 97.

3. *Serving the New Corporation* (Alexandria, VA: American Society for Training and Development, 1986).

4. Anthony Carnevale and Harold Goldstein, *Employee Training: Its Changing Role and An Analysis of New Data* (Alexandria, VA: American Society for Training and Development, 1983).

5. William Diehl and Larry Mikulecky, *Job Literacy* (Bloomington, IN: Indiana University School of Education, 1980).

6. U.S. Congress, Office of Technology Assessment, *Technology and Structural Unemployment: Reemploying Displaced Adults*, OTA-ITE-250 (Washington, DC: U.S. Government Printing Office, 1986), 64, 84.

Adult Literacy/Illiteracy in the United States

1

Chronology

THE FOLLOWING IS A CHRONOLOGY of significant events, legislation, and influences related to literacy and literacy education in the United States from colonial times to the present.

1647	Massachusetts passes the first compulsory school law in the New World, calling for the appointment of a teacher in every community of more than 50 families and for the establishment of a grammar school in every community of more than 100 families.
1713–1745	This 32-year period sees the founding of 22 newspapers in the colonies.
1777	First expenditure of federal funds for education, to provide instruction in mathematics and military skills to soldiers of the Continental Army.
1783	Publication of *Pennsylvania Evening Post,* the first daily newspaper in the United States, begins in Philadelphia.
1787	Publication of *Thoughts on Female Education* by Dr. Benjamin Rush provides evidence of a trend toward educating women.

Dr. Rush argued that the country must have well-educated mothers in order to have well-educated children.

1820   Establishment of first state-supported libraries in the United States, in New York and New Hampshire.

1821   First girls' high school in the United States founded by Emma H. Willard at Troy, New York.

1827   Massachusetts passes the first state high school law, mandating tax-supported high schools in communities of 500 or more families.

1833   First tax-supported library established at Petersborough, New Hampshire.

1836   First appearance of McGuffey's readers. The six readers will be revised five times, the last time in 1901, and will still be in use in 1927. McGuffey's readers will be the standard elementary school textbooks in most of the country for almost 100 years.

1837   Massachusetts establishes the first state board of education.

1840   U.S. Census includes literacy data for the first time; data gathering consists of asking heads of families how many white persons in the family over age 20 cannot read or write.

1845   Boston elementary schools are the first to use written examinations.

1850   U.S. Census Bureau bases its literacy data on asking individuals over 20 whether they can read or write.

        Annual distribution of newspapers in the United States rises to 22 per capita, compared to 8 per capita in 1828.

1852   Massachusetts passes first compulsory school attendance law, requiring all children between the ages of 8 and 14 to attend school a minimum of 12 weeks a year, 6 weeks of which must be consecutive. The penalty for noncompliance is $20.

1860   U.S. Census Bureau bases its literacy data on asking individuals over 20 whether they can read or write.

Department of Education survey finds 321 high schools in the United States, with over 50 percent of them in Massachusetts, New York, and Ohio.

1870   U.S. Census Bureau literacy data includes persons between 10 and 19 as well as those over 20; individuals are asked whether they can read *and* write.

1890   By this time, 27 states have compulsory school attendance laws.

1900   U.S. Census Bureau defines *illiterate* as a person 10 years of age or older unable to read and write in native language (asked as a yes/no question of individuals).

1911   Cora Wilson Stewart, superintendent of Rowan County, Kentucky, public schools, opens schools to adults on moonlit nights. The first session is held 5 September 1911, with volunteer teachers. The Moonlight Schools have an enrollment of some 1,200 adults, nearly all with no previous schooling. The sessions include drills in basic language, history, civics, agriculture, and sanitation concepts, and use a weekly newspaper, edited by Mrs. Stewart, in place of textbooks.

1912   The Moonlight Schools have spread to 12 counties and are serving 1,600 students. Other campaigns soon follow in South Carolina, Alabama, Oklahoma, Washington, Minnesota, and New Hampshire, with programs appearing later in Georgia, Mississippi, Arkansas, New York, Pennsylvania, and other states.

1913	New York City Workers Class Experiment seeks to provide elementary education for adults through the cooperation of the public schools (which provide teachers and equipment), industry (which provides space and time for students to attend without loss of wages), and individuals. The curriculum is similar to those that will be used in Adult Basic Education classes 50 years later. Participants improve both their efficiency and their hourly wages. Other factory classes are held in New Jersey, Ohio, Michigan, Pennsylvania, Illinois, and Massachusetts.
1914	With entry of the United States into World War I, the army finds that 25 percent of draftees are illiterate.
	The Moonlight Schools start special sessions for illiterate draftees; the campaign includes preparation of *The Soldier's First Book,* which includes explanations of why the United States is at war with Germany ("to keep our country free"). The Moonlight Schools effort leads to a government-sponsored literacy campaign, beginning at Camp Taylor, Kentucky, and spreading to other army camps.
	The success of the Moonlight Schools leads to the establishment of the first literacy commission, by Governor James McCreary of Kentucky. No funds are appropriated for its support, however.
	The Smith-Lever Act establishes the Cooperative Extension Service. This is the first major legislation to require the matching of federal and state, local, and/or institutional funds. It provides for grants to states for the purpose of helping persons not enrolled in school to understand and use effective practices in farming, marketing, family living, and community development.
1915	A literacy program is initiated in California by the State Department of Education, the

Immigration Commission, and the California Federation of Women's Clubs. Later in the year California passes a home teacher law allowing teachers to go from house to house to teach illiterates and others.

1917   After several efforts, Congress succeeds in passing (over President Wilson's veto) a bill requiring potential immigrants over age 16 to pass a literacy test showing that they can read in some language.

The Smith-Hughes Act provides for the support (through federal grants and matching state funds) of occupational training in agriculture, home economics, trades, and industries. Later amendments provide for training in health and office occupations, fishing, and technical skills used in national defense.

1918   By this time, all states have compulsory school attendance laws; three states will later repeal theirs (South Carolina in 1955, Mississippi in 1956, Virginia in 1959).

Passage of the Immigration and Nationality Act provides federal funds to assist public schools in providing English language, history, government, and citizenship programs for immigrants who are candidates for naturalization.

1919   National Education Association (NEA) calls for compulsory school attendance to at least age 18. Utah had passed a law to that effect earlier in the year, but few states followed suit (four by 1960). Three other states specified an upper limit of 17.

1920   U.S. Census Bureau defines *illiterate* as any person 10 years of age or over unable to write in any language, regardless of ability to read.

The National Education Association (NEA) organizes a Department of Immigrant Education, which later expands to include native illiterates and changes its name to the National Department of Adult Education of the NEA.

1921   The On-Reservation Indian Adult Education Program is established to provide literacy training for Indians. About 30,000 Indians in 190 communities will participate.

1924   The Sterling-Reed Bill seeks to create a department of education, with a specifically stated goal being research into and efforts to "remove" illiteracy. The bill, which does not pass, calls for appropriations to states for instruction of illiterates aged 14 and over; it also includes provisions for programs to teach English to immigrants.

An illiteracy conference is held in January in Washington, DC, with representatives from each state, several organizations (including the General Federation of Women's Clubs and the American Legion), and the national government. The purpose of the conference is to formulate programs for literacy work in the United States. Overall it produces little in the way of direct action; a conference committee to design a course of study and instructional methods does result in a Bureau of Education bulletin, *Elementary Instruction for Adults,* which details curriculum approaches and materials for native-born illiterates.

1925   The Commission of Education conducts a National Survey of State Programs of Adult Education, with 44 of 48 states responding: 34 states have passed legislation dealing with adult education; 24 give some financial support to adult education programs; 27 provide leadership through their state departments of education; and 25 have approximately 286,000 students in classes for adult illiterates and the foreign-born.

1927   By this time, most states have passed laws encouraging adult education. For example, California requires illiterates between the ages of 18 and 21 to attend school and has a literacy test for voters; Connecticut requires school districts with over 10,000 residents to maintain evening schools for persons over 14.

1929   President Herbert Hoover appoints an Advisory Committee on National Illiteracy to research literacy education and the factors influencing illiteracy and to advise the National Advisory Committee on Education. On 17 December, the committee initiates a national literacy campaign with the goal of offering five million adults the opportunity to learn to read and write before the 1930 census. The campaign is to accomplish this goal with $50,000 in funds, all from private contributions.

1930   The National Education Association (NEA) decides that literacy programs should aim at student achievement of sixth-grade reading level as a basis for literacy.

1933   Myles Horton founds the Highlander Folk School in Ozone, Tennessee. Although not specifically concerned with literacy, the school is an innovator in providing adult education that meets real and felt needs. Its purpose is to serve the educational needs of local mountain people by teaching not from books, but from the life, works, culture, and history of the Cumberland Mountains and the South. The Highlander Folk School will teach adults how to participate in such social movements as the labor organizations of the 1930s, the civil rights movement of the 1950s and 1960s, and the Appalachian poverty programs of the 1960s.

Under President Franklin D. Roosevelt the government initiates several employment-related educational programs. Three of these include provisions for literacy and/or basic skills training: the Federal Emergency Relief Administration (FERA), which includes funds and programs for keeping schools open, teaching English, and providing general adult education; the Works Progress Administration (WPA), which includes provisions for literacy and citizenship education in addition to college-level academic education; and the Civilian Conservation Corps (CCC), which includes basic education programs for semiliterate and illiterate participants.

1936   A four-year literacy campaign is begun by the Works Progress Administration (WPA), in conjunction with various social agencies and the New York City Board of Education. WPA will enlarge the program in 1938, saying over one million people have been taught to read and write.

1940   U.S. Census Bureau, instead of asking individuals whether they can read and write, collects data on the highest number of school grades completed.

1945   High illiteracy rates among draftees lead to development of literacy instruction materials by the military. The materials, which include filmstrips, texts, and workbooks, represent the first large-scale effort to provide materials designed for teaching adults. They take a functional approach, introducing skills and materials related to military life. Sample titles include *The Story of Private Pete, A Soldier's General Orders,* and *How to Wear Your Uniform.*

1946   The American Association on Adult Education, the National Conference on Adult Education and the Negro, and the U.S. Office of Education initiate the Project for Adult Education of Negroes, with the goal of raising the educational level of black functional illiterates. The project, financed primarily by grants from the Carnegie Corporation of New York and directed by Ambrose Caliver, is the only major civilian literacy effort to occur during the 1940s.

1947 For the first time, the U.S. Census Bureau collects specific data on literacy. The study, which bases its statistics on highest grade completed, assumes that most illiterates will be those with less than five years of school, and conversely, that persons who have completed five years or more of school are literate. The study sees the first use of the term *functional illiterate,* defined as a person who has completed fewer than five years of elementary school.

1949 The U.S. Army establishes schools for teaching illiterate draftees. The army will report that 257,000 illiterates were brought to fifth-grade level between 1949 and 1954, through a program requiring seven to eight months of each draftee's two-year term of service.

1950 In the first year of the Korean War, approximately 300,000 men, the majority of them from Southern states, are rejected for military service due to educational deficiencies.

1952 The Adult Education Association of the United States sets up an investigative committee on adult and fundamental education.

1955 The U.S. Office of Education establishes an Adult Education Section.

Frank C. Laubach founds Laubach Literacy International (LLI). LLI bases its approach on the Laubach Method, using alphabet/picture associations and phonetic symbols, and employs a worldwide network of volunteers working under the philosophy of "Each One Teach One."

1956 The Library Service Act provides for public library programs for rural adults.

1957　　The Adult Education Association of the United States establishes the National Commission for Adult Literacy. The commission is a nongovernment agency formed to encourage federal, state, and local governments—through public awareness programs, conferences, and publications—to provide all adults with the opportunity to gain basic reading, writing, and arithmetic skills. The commission will be disbanded in 1961.

For the first time, television is used to teach illiterates. The goal of the program, developed and broadcast by WKNO-TV in Memphis, Tennessee, is to bring students to fourth-grade level in 350 hours of instruction. The instruction consists of 98 half-hour televised lessons (3 per week), supplemented by volunteer-supervised homework in viewing/reading centers. The Laubach Method–based program will be credited with bringing 2,000 people to functional literacy (a figure that represented 3 percent of the target group) in two years. WKNO-TV packages the series of lessons for distribution to other TV stations around the country.

Baylor University in Waco, Texas, is the first university to offer a literacy studies curriculum, in response to a speech by former president Dwight Eisenhower stressing the need for an established college-level program. Based on the methods developed by Frank Laubach, the Baylor program becomes a model and stimulus for literacy work in Texas and around the country. In 1963, the program will be transferred to the Department of Journalism in cooperation with the Department of Religion. It will be allowed to die, apparently from lack of funding, after the 1968–1969 school year.

1959   Raymond M. Hilliard, director of public aid for Cook County, Illinois, starts a program to teach 50,000 relief recipients to read and write. The program is initially paid for by the Chicago Board of Education and later receives federal and state funds. It was inspired by a perceived link between poverty and illiteracy, based on a study of the Woodlawn neighborhood, where 25 percent of households were on relief and 51 percent of the able-bodied adults could not read or write above fifth-grade level. The program's biggest problem is child care.

A U.S. Census Bureau survey finds rates of illiteracy (defined as an inability to read and write a simple message in any language) highest among the older, the unemployed, farm workers, laborers, and Southerners. The survey indicated that "a great proportion of [the remaining native white] illiterates were probably unable to learn to read and write because of physical or mental deficiencies" (Cook 1977, 66).

By this time, every state except Kansas has passed laws regarding the provision of adult education.

1961   The "Operation Alphabet" television series is developed by Philadelphia Public School Extension Division, produced by WFIL-TV, and distributed without charge to television stations by the National Association for Public School Adult Education. The series consists of 100 half-hour lessons in basic reading and writing skills broadcast over 20 weeks; it is supplemented by a home study book. Each week's lessons include four days of new words and one script letter, followed by a one-day review. The series, whose goal is to bring viewers to a third-grade level and encourage them to continue learning by enrolling in adult education classes, will have been televised in over 100 communities by 1966.

1962   Congress passes the Manpower Develop-
            ment and Training Act (MDTA) program.
            The program's goal is to retrain 400,000 un-
            employed and underemployed persons in
            three years. It is intended as a partnership
            between the Department of Labor and the
            Department of Health, Education, and Wel-
            fare. The discovery that large numbers of
            unemployed individuals are untrainable
            because of a lack of basic literacy skills leads
            to two amendments to the act: the first pro-
            vides for further schooling for 17- to 21-
            year-old youth who lack the skills necessary
            for occupational training; the second pro-
            vides for basic education for adults without
            the educational skills to profit from occupa-
            tional training. The training provides a
            $20/week "allowance" to youth trainees and
            $10/week over the amount allowed for un-
            employment compensation for adults, for a
            maximum period of 72 weeks. The cost for
            the first two years is to be paid for by con-
            gressional appropriations, with the pro-
            grams developed locally (a few at state
            level).

            A study of relief recipients conducted by Dr.
            Denton J. Brooks shows that grade comple-
            tion does not necessarily indicate a corre-
            sponding level of achievement (Cook 1977,
            97–98). When Chicago institutes a citywide
            program to address the problem, only 7,000
            of an estimated 270,000 potential enrollees
            show up.

            At this time, only 19 states have one or more
            professional staff members working in adult
            education; New York is the only state with a
            full-time professional for adult literacy and
            basic skills programs.

1963   The Vocational Education Act recognizes
            the need for integration of vocational and
            general education. Its objectives include the
            provision of high school programs designed
            to decrease the dropout rate as well as pro-

grams for dropouts and high school graduates needing additional occupational training and adults needing to upgrade job skills. In addition to training, the act provides for counseling and guidance services. It also includes funds for building vocational schools and occupational departments in established public institutions.

The Library Service Act is intended to augment the number of people using public libraries and to facilitate purchase of trade publications and instructional materials; it includes provisions for construction of facilities and increases the annual federal authorization from $7.5 million to $25 million.

The National Defense Education Act includes an amendment that provides for funding of research and demonstration projects in educational media by educational institutions and nonprofit educational organizations. The intent of the act is that textbook and trade publishers will work with institutions to solve mutual problems.

Public Law 531 permits funding of basic research, demonstrations, developmental activities, and reviews by state departments of education and colleges and universities. The U.S. Office of Education seeks proposals related to dealing with problems of the uneducated and undereducated through research and demonstration centers. The centers will develop instructional materials and act as field testing centers for evaluating the materials. They will also prepare suitable reading materials for processing and marketing by trade book publishers.

Amendments to the Social Security Act create the Community Work and Training Programs under the Welfare Administration of the Department of Health, Education, and Welfare. The programs are federally funded and operated through local school districts. They are intended to provide basic education and occupational training to welfare recipients. Participants are to continue to receive welfare payments while they gain enough education to become employable and get off welfare.

1964   An interdisciplinary conference at the Center for Applied Linguistics in Washington, DC, recognizes the need for research in organizing and administering literacy programs.

The Economic Opportunity Act initiates the Adult Basic Education (ABE) program for adults 16 and over who have less than 12 years of schooling and who are not currently enrolled in public school. ABE allots funds to the states and six territories, which in turn fund local public and private programs. This is the first time the federal government has allotted funds directly for literacy instruction.

Funds available under the Library Services and Construction Act stimulate delivery of library services to adults who are economically and socially disadvantaged, handicapped, home-bound, or institutionalized.

1965   The Ford Foundation sponsors the Inter-University Workshop on Adult Basic Education to train adult basic education teachers, with the intent that they will go home and train others. The workshop's curriculum is similar to that offered by Baylor University.

1966   The Adult Education Act establishes Adult Basic Education (ABE) under the Office of Education. The program's stated goals emphasize the transmission of literacy and other basic skills as a means of increasing employability and enabling adults to function as productive members of society. Later amendments will add programs for teaching English as a Second Language (ESL) and for adults in correctional institutions, hospitals, and other custodial settings.

The Adult Education Act also establishes and provides funds for the National Teacher Training Adult Basic Education Program, a national council that is to prepare a curriculum for teacher training used in institutes around the country—9 in 1966, 19 in 1967, 27 (in 24 states) in 1968, 20 in 1970. The summer institutes consist of a three-week teacher training program and a two-week administration program. Participants receive full tuition, stipend, and travel expenses; they are intended to develop skills that they can return to their communities.

The Defense Department institutes Project 100,000, aimed at assisting efforts to raise the educational level of disadvantaged individuals. The project uses tutoring, special training, and counseling to bring an experimental group of individuals who scored low on an entrance exam to a point where they compare favorably with a higher-scoring control group in basic training, skills training, promotions, and overall service performance. The program has an average cost of $200 per man.

UNESCO declares 8 September International Literacy Day, "to draw international attention to the importance of literacy for all peoples."

1968 The annual report on Adult Basic Education (ABE) programs shows 456,000 adults involved during the fiscal year, an increase of 17 percent over 1967. About 50 percent of enrollees are white, 43 percent black, the rest "non-white." The report also shows that more than 60 percent of states provided funds in addition to matching funds needed to qualify for federal aid.

By this time, there are 32 institutes producing literacy teachers and 21 Special

Experimental Demonstration Projects (compared to 13 in 1967) working to identify effective adult basic education materials, curriculum designs, and administrative systems.

1969   The U.S. Census Bureau survey bases literacy statistics on grade completion, with the assumption that anyone who has completed six years of school is literate.

The Adult Education Act amends the Adult Basic Education Act of 1966 to extend benefits to persons with less than a twelfth-grade education, raising the number of potential participants from 24 to 69 million. It also provides funds for Adult Basic Education (ABE) programs and related teacher training, research, and administration projects.

The Right to Read program is funded, with the stated goal of eradicating illiteracy by the end of the decade. The program is intended to stimulate public and private efforts within the states to improve reading skills among the entire population. It includes two adult-oriented programs: community-based programs for adults 16 and over, and reading academies.

1971   The Adult Performance Level (APL) study begins in Austin, Texas. Sponsored by the U.S. Department of Education, the APL is the first to attempt to categorize and measure "functional competence," defined as the ability to use skills and knowledge needed to meet the requirements for adult living. The list of competencies developed through the study will become the basis for competency-based adult education programs around the country.

1974   Education amendments further extend the Elementary and Secondary Act of 1965, with the aim of strengthening reading instruction for all groups. The amendments provide for the establishment of reading academies by colleges or universities and nonprofit organizations to teach reading to youths and adults who would not otherwise receive such instruction.

1975   *Adult Functional Competency: a Summary,* detailing the results of the Adult Performance Level (APL) study, is published by the Adult Performance Level Project.

1979   The Ford Foundation sponsors World Education Inc.'s landmark study on illiteracy in the United States. The study culminates in the publication of *Adult Illiteracy in the United States* by Carman St. John Hunter with David Harman (revised 1985).

1983   President Ronald Reagan, at the urging of Secretary of Education Terrel Bell, establishes the Adult Literacy Initiative under the Division of Adult Education of the U.S. Department of Education. The initiative's fourfold objective is to (1) generate national awareness; (2) promote public/private sector partnerships and encourage volunteerism; (3) provide technical and networking assistance; and (4) coordinate federal literacy activities within the Department of Education and with other departments and agencies.

As part of the Adult Literacy Initiative, the National Institute of Education sponsors the National Adult Literacy Project. The goal of the 2½-year project is to assemble and report current information on literacy issues through a combination of information dissemination and technical assistance, research and development, and policy analysis. Project activities include developing an organizing model for literacy programs, collecting information from existing programs, and holding a national two-day conference on literacy instruction (1984).

B. Dalton Bookseller launches its National Literacy Initiative, a four-year program to reduce illiteracy through direct grants, leadership, advocacy, and assistance. The program includes $3 million in grants to literacy programs; funding for resource development, including literacy program management software, handbooks, and reports; consultation; technical assistance; and promotional and recruitment efforts, including participation in the Coalition for Literacy's national advertising campaign. The project will end in 1986, having spawned two additional projects, the Urban Literacy Development Fund and the Give the Gift of Literacy Foundation.

In November, the Contact Literacy Center toll-free national hotline begins taking calls. By June 1987, the hotline will have handled over 200,000 calls, many of them inspired by the Project Literacy U.S. (PLUS) campaign, which begins in September 1986. Just over 59 percent of the calls are from potential volunteers; 32 percent are from potential students; the remainder are for general information or other requests.

1985 The first national Conference on Adult Literacy and Computers is held in Spring Hill, Minnesota. The conference is attended by leaders representing a range of literacy instruction providers from around the country. Long-term goals of the conference are to support the development of computer use in adult literacy programs and to create an effective dissemination system for information on computers and other forms of technology, hardware and software selection, training, curriculum design, evaluation, and organizational recommendations for adult literacy programs.

1986 The National Assessment of Educational Progress (NAEP) releases *Literacy: Profiles* *of America's Young Adults*. The report details the results of the NAEP study of literacy skills of 21- to 25-year-olds. It concludes that most young adults have basic literacy skills but lack "critical thinking" skills.

Governor Gerald Baililes of Virginia announces a "no reading, no release" policy requiring state prison inmates to be literate before they can be paroled.

The U.S. Congress declares the week of 20 April 1986 as "National Reading Is Fun Week," 2 July 1986 as "National Literacy Day," September 1986 as "Adult Literacy Awareness Month," and 1987 as the "Year of the Reader." The 99th Congress also amends the Job Training Partnership Act to require funding for illiteracy and dropout prevention programs and establishes the Literacy Corps as part of the Volunteers in Service to America (VISTA) program.

In September, the American Broadcasting Company (ABC) and Public Broadcasting Service (PBS) networks launch a national media outreach literacy program, Project Literacy U.S. (PLUS). The PLUS effort, which includes documentary broadcasts, multimedia advertising, and public service announcements, results in an onslaught of calls to local hotlines and to the toll-free number at the Contact Literacy Center.

1987   At the request of the Library of Congress, Congress passes a resolution designating 1987 as the "Year of the Reader." The resolution calls for encouraging activities "aimed at restoring the act of reading to a place of preeminence in our personal lives and in the life of the nation." Plans include a commemorative stamp, posters, and at least one traveling exhibit. "Year of the Reader" is also adopted as a theme by the International Reading Association and the American Booksellers Association, among others. The

Center for the Book at the Library of Congress plans to continue the promotion with a new theme through at least 1988.

The Project Literacy U.S. (PLUS) campaign is renewed through May 1988. The second year focuses on three themes: "civic literacy," "literacy in the workforce," and "literacy and youth." Plans include public service announcements by "learners of the month," news, documentary and made-for-TV movie presentations, and outreach activities such as teleconferences. The goals of one such teleconference, sponsored by PLUS, the American Association of Community and Junior Colleges, and IBM Educational Systems, among others, include "conquering illiteracy by the year 2000."

In June, the first national Conference on Adult Literacy and Technology is held at the University of Pennsylvania. It draws over 300 participants, who attend presentations on such topics as evolving technology, instruction, and software.

In September, the first National Adult Literacy Congress is held in Philadelphia as part of the We the People 200 bicentennial celebration of the Constitution. All 52 delegates—one from each of the fifty states, Washington, DC, and Puerto Rico—are students or former students in adult literacy programs and were chosen by local literacy organizations to represent their states. The Congress develops positions on six topics chosen by a steering committee of students: (1) Who We Are, Educating the Public about Literacy; (2) Literacy and the Workplace; (3) Legislation, Funding, and Resources for Literacy; (4) Our Involvement in Issues of Literacy; (5) Literacy for Non–English Speaking Adults; and (6) What's Worked for Us.

1990   International Literacy Year, sponsored by UNESCO.

2

Biographical Sketches

THE FOLLOWING ARE BRIEF BIOGRAPHICAL sketches of individuals who play or have played a key role in the understanding and promotion of adult literacy in the United States. They include researchers, theorists, authors, spokespersons, activists, and innovative program designers and developers. They also include persons who, by virtue of their positions, are likely to have a significant effect on the current and future direction of literacy theory and practice.

Like all such lists, this one is necessarily subjective and incomplete. There are many people, far too many to include here—researchers, writers, spokespersons, program initiators and directors, and thousands of teachers, volunteers, and others—who have contributed time, energy, imagination, and insight to various literacy-related efforts. The persons cited here are representative of that greater whole.

Eunice N. Askov (1940–)

Eunice Askov is the director of the Institute for the Study of Adult Literacy, an innovative, multifaceted program that is seeking, among other goals, to broaden and strengthen the research base for literacy efforts. Dr. Askov began her career as a high school

23

English and reading teacher, and later taught adult basic education before becoming involved in reading and literacy research and program development. She served on the Studies and Research Committee of the International Reading Association and was a Fulbright scholar to the University of Western Australia, where she developed computer-based adult literacy courseware. She has been a program cochair on the board of directors of the American Reading Forum and currently chairs the National Steering Committee for the Adult Literacy and Technology Project, which is being coordinated by the institute.

Dr. Askov, who received her doctorate from the University of Wisconsin–Madison in 1969, has been a presenter at a number of international, regional, and state conferences on reading, literacy, and adult education. She is a professor of education at Pennsylvania State University, where the institute is based.

PUBLICATIONS: *Meeting the Challenge: Creative Reading Instruction in the Classroom* (1985), *Content-Area Reading: An Individualized Approach* (1982), plus several book chapters, various teacher and student reading materials, and articles in professional journals and yearbooks.

Terrel H. Bell (1921–)

Terrel Bell has been a leader in education for more than 20 years. He began his professional career as a science teacher and athletic coach in a rural Idaho high school after World War II and subsequently served as superintendent in school districts in Idaho, Wyoming, and Utah, becoming Utah's state superintendent in 1963. His involvement on a national level began in 1970, when he became deputy commissioner for school systems in the U.S. Office of Education. In 1974, he became U.S. commissioner of education, serving in that position through 1976.

Dr. Bell is probably best known for his leadership role with the National Commission on Excellence in Education, which produced "A Nation at Risk," a hard-hitting report that helped focus attention on some critical problems in U.S. public education. Twelve million copies of the report have been printed and disseminated since its release. As secretary of education under

Ronald Reagan, Dr. Bell was instrumental in establishing the Adult Literacy Initiative. Dr. Bell resigned as secretary of education in 1986. He has returned to Utah, where he is serving as professor of educational administration at the University of Utah.

Dr. Bell, who received his doctorate in educational administration from the University of Utah, has also been awarded 21 honorary doctorates. He often speaks at various conferences around the country, and continues to be an advocate of and an important voice in education in the United States.

PUBLICATIONS: Published works include *A Philosophy of Education for the Space Age* (1960), *Active Parent Concern* (1974), the first chapter of *Excellence* (1984), plus various articles.

Barbara Bush (1925–)

Although Barbara Bush is active in a number of volunteer organizations, she has made reading and literacy her primary focus, taking a national leadership role in literacy efforts. She is a sponsor of Laubach Literacy International, serves on the national board of Reading Is Fundamental, is honorary chair of the National Advisory Council of Literacy Volunteers of America, and serves on the board of directors of the Business Council for Effective Literacy. She is also an honorary member of the board of the Kingsbury Center, a Washington, DC–based organization for children with learning disabilities. Mrs. Bush speaks frequently around the country on behalf of literacy efforts, taking advantage of her role as wife of the vice president of the United States to gain widespread public attention for her message. In 1984, Mrs. Bush published a collection of anecdotes about the family's late cocker spaniel; she is donating all proceeds from the book, *C. Fred's Story,* to Laubach Literacy Action and Literacy Volunteers of America.

Mrs. Bush's recent honors include the 1983 Woman of the Year Award from the Women's National Republican Club, the United Negro College Fund Distinguished Leadership Award (1986), and the Distinguished American Woman Award (1987).

Ruth Johnson Colvin*

Ruth Colvin is the founder of Literacy Volunteers of America, a national organization of over 200 local and state programs providing tutor training, technical assistance, and support to nonprofessional, volunteer basic skills and English for Speakers of Other Languages (ESOL) tutors. Mrs. Colvin began her volunteer recruitment and training program in her basement in 1962, after realizing that more than 11,000 adults in her home county of Onondaga, New York, could not read or write. Within four years, her volunteer program had expanded to communities around the state. In 1967, the program was incorporated as the Literacy Volunteers of America (LVA); affiliates now exist in over 30 states.

A primary component of LVA's approach is intensive training and ongoing support of tutors. Originally, Mrs. Colvin used existing materials for training and tutoring; when these proved inadequate, she developed her own. LVA now provides a wide range of printed and audiovisual materials for both tutors and students. As chair of research and development for LVA, Mrs. Colvin continues to work on the development of effective materials for teaching basic reading and conversational English. She also continues to lecture and holds workshops throughout the world, promoting both literacy and her belief that well-trained and supervised volunteers can be effective tutors.

Among Ruth Colvin's numerous honors are the National Volunteer Award for Distinguished Service (1972), Woman of Achievement Post Standard All Time Award (1986 and 1964), the American Association of University Women's Woman of Accomplishment award (1987), and the White House–President's Volunteer Award (1987). Mrs. Colvin has also received honorary doctorates from the State University of New York, Marymount College, and Syracuse University.

PUBLICATIONS: *Leader,* handbook for community organizers; *Tutor,* handbook for tutors of basic reading (coauthor); *Read* test, basic reading test for adults and teenagers (coauthor); *I Speak English,* handbook for ESOL tutors; slide/tape training workshops for basic reading and ESOL tutors; *A Way with Words,* story of LVA; *Tutoring Small Groups: Basic Reading* (contributing author).

*birthdate not available

Helen (Jinx) Crouch*

Helen (Jinx) Crouch has been the national director of Literacy Volunteers of America (LVA) since 1981, and recently became the organization's president as well. Ms. Crouch started as a volunteer tutor in 1969, using techniques learned in one of LVA's basic reading workshops. Her involvement soon deepened, and within a few years she had become a key member of LVA's administrative organization. She joined the board of directors in 1971, serving as its president from 1972 to 1974, when she was named assistant director of field services. In 1979 she was promoted to director of field services, becoming executive director two years later. Under Ms. Crouch's leadership, Literacy Volunteers of America has grown considerably both in membership and in recognition of its role as a major national force in literacy efforts.

Ms. Crouch is a charter member and chairman of the Program Response Committee of the Coalition for Literacy and has served as a consultant/trainer for the American Library Association's literacy training project. Ms. Crouch has also played key roles in other social service organizations, including the Volunteer Bureau of Rochester (New York) and the National Council on Alcoholism.

*birthdate not available

Paul V. Delker (1927–)

Paul Delker has been involved in adult education for more than 30 years, 25 of them at a national level. From 1966 to 1986, he directed the Division of Adult Education at the U.S. Department of Education. During that period, he was responsible for directing programs that extended the resources of universities, colleges, and public school systems for educating adults, particularly those who were deficient in basic skills and/or who lacked high school diplomas. Under the Adult Education Act of 1966, Mr. Delker managed a $10 million annual national discretionary program and $102 million in grants to states, directing the development of a program that serves almost three million adults annually and that includes over 4,000 educational sites in business and industry. He also developed legislative amendments, regulations and policies for implementing the Adult Education Act and other federal legislation, and represented the United States at UNESCO gatherings on adult education in 1972, 1976, and 1981.

Prior to his tenure at the Division of Adult Education, Mr. Delker served as deputy director for the University Relations and Training Division of the Peace Corps (1962–1966). Before coming to Washington in 1962, he worked in personnel research and executive development at Sandia National Laboratory in New Mexico, and served as a personnel director for two corporations in South Bend, Indiana.

Mr. Delker is president of Strategic Education Systems, a MacLean, Virginia–based organization designed to address ways in which environments developed for purposes other than learning can improve their efficiency and effectiveness by adopting learning as a principle around which work and life are organized. He is an advisor to the Business Council for Effective Literacy and has served as a faculty member or guest lecturer at several universities, including Harvard and Columbia.

Mr. Delker's recent honors include the National Council of State Directors of Adult Education Leadership Award (1986); the Outstanding Adult Educator Award from the Commission of Adult Basic Education (1981); nominee for the Presidential Award for Outstanding Service (by Secretary of Education Terrel Bell, 1982); *Who's Who in the East* (1983–1986); and *Who's Who in Education* (1983–1986).

PUBLICATIONS: *The New Literacy: Adult Education as Public Policy* (1988); plus book chapters, articles, reports, and papers.

Karl O. Haigler (1948–   )

Although a relative newcomer to the literacy field, Karl Haigler is in a position to have a significant impact in adult education and literacy efforts nationwide during the coming years. A former high school principal, consultant, and teacher, Mr. Haigler has been director of the Department of Education's Adult Literacy Initiative since 1985; in 1986, he took over the Division of Adult

Education as well. These two programs represent the primary focus of the federal government's role in funding, assisting, and promoting efforts to provide instruction in literacy and other basic skills to disadvantaged adults.

While a high school principal, Karl Haigler was the only secondary school member to serve on the panel for the National Endowment for the Humanities Chairman's Report on the Humanities in Higher Education, *To Reclaim a Legacy* (1984). His school was one of 60 private secondary school programs designated by the Council of American Private Education as "exemplary" as part of the U.S. Department of Education's secondary school recognition program (1983–1984).

Jean E. Hammink (1949–)

Jean Hammink was instrumental in the development of and served as director for B. Dalton Bookseller's National Literacy Initiative, a $3 million, four-year project that provided program and management consultation, developed funding and support resources, and participated in a number of partnership projects, including the Coalition for Literacy. The initiative succeeded in generating considerable national attention for literacy efforts. Ms. Hammink has been involved with literacy work since 1974, when she coordinated a reading program and inmate tutor program at a maximum security prison in Moberly, Missouri. In 1977, she became director of the Minnesota Literacy Council, a statewide volunteer organization that trained and supported more than 2,000 volunteers through 100 local projects. Ms. Hammink first became involved in national literacy efforts in 1982, as a consultant to B. Dalton Bookseller's Community Giving program. She now directs the Urban Literacy Development Fund, an organization that grew out of the B. Dalton Initiative and that provides grants, communication, training, and advocacy in support of literacy efforts in urban areas around the country.

Ms. Hammink has served on a number of national literacy committees and task forces, including Laubach Literacy Action's long-range planning and public policy committees, Literacy Volunteers of America (LVA) field services committee, the Adult

Literacy Initiative Task Force, and the National Coalition for Literacy's executive and campaign response committees. She is also on the national advisory boards for the Institute for the Study of Adult Literacy, the Adult Literacy and Technology Network, ACTION's Retired Senior Volunteer Program (RSVP) Literacy Project, and the National Issues Forum (NIF) Literacy Project. Between 1982 and 1987, she spoke on literacy at approximately 100 national, state, and local conferences.

David Harman (1944–)

David Harman is a learning theorist and researcher who also works on the practical aspects of literacy program implementation. He first became involved in literacy programs in the late 1960s in his native Israel, where he directed a national adult literacy program, supervising a corps of 1,000 teachers, 30 supervisors, and 4 regional offices serving 35,000 students a year. In that role, he was also responsible for developing curricula, producing a weekly newspaper, and all training activities. Since the early 1970s, he has served as a consultant on literacy and adult education for the U.S. Department of Education, World Education, the World Bank, the U.S. Institute for International Development, and the Harvard Institute for International Development. He was a consultant in the design of the Adult Performance Level (APL) study, and is currently a consultant to the Business Council for Effective Literacy. He has authored a number of significant works on literacy, including the 1979 Ford Foundation study, *Adult Illiteracy in the United States* (with Carman St. John Hunter), and the more recent *Illiteracy: A National Dilemma* and *What Works in Adult Literacy*, the latter produced for the Adult Literacy Initiative at the U.S. Department of Education.

Dr. Harman earned his doctorate in education from Harvard University in 1971 and has served on the faculties of Harvard and the Hebrew University of Jerusalem. He is currently a visiting professor of education at Columbia University and is president of the Institute for Corporate Education, which specializes in working with corporations to develop education and training programs.

PUBLICATIONS: Books include *Community Fundamental Education* (1974); *Adult Illiteracy in the United States* (1979 and 1985, with Carman St. John Hunter); *Illiteracy: A National Dilemma* (1987); and *What Works in Adult Literacy* (1987). Other publications include several monographs and numerous articles and book chapters on the subjects of illiteracy and adult education.

Malcolm S. Knowles (1913–)

Although not directly concerned with literacy education, Malcolm Knowles is widely recognized as a leader in the field of adult learning, in which he has been involved for nearly 40 years. Dr. Knowles, who received his doctorate from the University of Chicago in 1960, pioneered many of the concepts and methods of *andragogy*, a term he coined to denote the education of adults. Currently professor emeritus of adult and community college education at North Carolina State University, Dr. Knowles is also a mentor for the Human and Organization Development Faculty at the Fielding Institute in Santa Barbara, California, and has served on the faculty of Boston University. He has been a consultant and workshop leader for numerous corporations, including General Electric, IBM, AT&T, Dupont, and Polaroid, as well as for universities, churches and dioceses, civic organizations, and government agencies in many countries. He was executive director of the Adult Education Association of the U.S.A. (now the American Association for Adult and Continuing Education) from 1951 through 1959.

Among Dr. Knowles's many honors are Adult Educator of the Year Award from the Committee on Social Justice, International Women's Year, National Association for Public Continuing and Adult Education (1975); Outstanding Educators of America (1975); and the Research-to-Practice Award, Adult Education Association of the U.S.A. (1979). He is also the recipient of several honorary doctorates.

PUBLICATIONS: Dr. Knowles has published 13 books, including *The Modern Practice of Adult Education* (1970, rev. 1980); *The Adult Learner: A Neglected Species* (1973, rev. 1978 and 1984); *A History of the Adult Education Movement in the U.S.* (1977); *Andragogy in Action* (1984); and *Using Learning Contracts* (1986). He is the author of numerous articles, reviews, and book chapters, and has been involved in several media productions on adult learning for educational and public television and corporate training programs.

Judith Ann Koloski (1944–)

Since 1985, Judith Koloski has been the Executive Director of the American Association for Adult and Continuing Education (AAACE), the largest professional association of adult educators in the United States. Ms. Koloski came to the AAACE with an impressive record in adult and continuing education, including a period as executive director of Literacy Volunteers of America (LVA) for Connecticut. As state director of adult and community education in Maryland, she was one of the most active and visible state directors in the country, serving two AAACE chairmanships and becoming a respected and vocal advocate for adult education at both the state and federal levels.

In pursuit of her goals of strengthening policy development, collaboration, and professionalism for the field of adult education, Ms. Koloski works with policy makers and other national and state organizations, including the Gannett Foundation's Task Force on Adult Illiteracy and the National Governors Association. She also testifies frequently on behalf of adult education issues at state and federal hearings. Under her leadership, the AAACE has grown in membership and influence and has become an increasingly important force in all aspects of adult education, including literacy efforts.

Ms. Koloski's recent honors include being declared the "1987 Person of the Year—Outside the Field" by the National Council on Community Services and Continuing Education, an affiliate of the American Association of Community and Junior Colleges.

Jonathan Kozol (1936–)

Jonathan Kozol, a nationally known author and speaker, is an often-controversial figure who, as an independent with no program to protect, can afford to be more vocal than others who are involved with literacy efforts. He is determined and passionate and he gets attention. One of his primary goals is convincing the federal government to make greater efforts to combat illiteracy, a mission that frequently puts him at odds with officials. His free hand with statistics and his opposition to certain approaches, such as the use of technology in adult literacy instruction, have likewise put him at odds with others in the field. Nonetheless, he is a powerful speaker and a tireless crusader with an ability to raise issues, rouse emotions, and inspire action as well as talk. His efforts have attracted people in academia, government, business, and public education to the cause of literacy, and his books have provoked public discussion and focused attention on adult illiteracy as an issue.

A Rhodes scholar and recipient of several fellowships, including Saxton, Guggenheim, the Field Foundation, and the Ford Foundation, Mr. Kozol has taught public school in Boston, been a visiting lecturer at Yale University, and consulted for the U.S. Office of Education. His teaching experiences were the inspiration for his first book, *Death at an Early Age,* which won a National Book Award in 1968 and made him a well-known author. Mr. Kozol, who has recently softened his stance on some issues such as the use of computers to teach reading, continues to fight for literacy through numerous public speaking engagements and through his writing. He also consults with various literacy groups around the country.

PUBLICATIONS: *Death at an Early Age* (1967); *Free Schools* (1972); *The Night Is Dark and I Am Far from Home* (1975); *Prisoners of Science: Breaking the Bonds of Adult Illiteracy in the United States* (1980); *Illiterate America* (1985).

Martha A. Lane (1942–)

As head of the Lutheran Church Women's (LCW) Volunteer Reading Program, Martha Lane earned a reputation for "cutting across the lines" separating various literacy groups and issues. She also became known as a student advocate, supporting the rights of adult literacy students to have a say in the policies and practices that affect their lives. In addition to coordinating LCW's literacy and English for Speakers of Other Language (ESOL) programs at a national level, Ms. Lane has conducted workshops for new tutors, assisted communities in setting up literacy programs, worked with other denominations and organizations in literacy projects, and conducted leadership training and other literacy-related seminars and workshops. She is a member of the Long Range Planning Committee for Laubach Literacy Action and of the National Steering Committee for the Adult Literacy and Technology Project, and serves as a consultant to the Mayor's Commission on Literacy in Philadelphia, the California State Library Literacy Campaign, the Business Council for Effective Literacy, and other groups.

In late 1987, the Lutheran Church Women merged with the Women of the Evangelical Lutheran Church in America, eliminating Ms. Lane's position. Although her exact role was uncertain at the time of this book's publication, Martha Lane will undoubtedly continue to be an important voice in the field.

Ms. Lane's major awards include the 1976 Outstanding Contribution in the Area of Education award from the National Affiliation for Literacy Advance and the first annual Literacy Award presented by the Philadelphia chapter of the International Reading Association in 1983. In 1984, she was recognized by the U.S. Department of Education for her outstanding contribution to adult literacy efforts.

PUBLICATIONS: Books include *The Laubach Way to English,* ESOL teacher's manuals (coauthor, 1976); *Handbook for Volunteer Reading Aides* (rev. 1975 and 1984); *Emergency English: A Handbook for Tutors of Non–English Speaking Adults* (1979, rev. 1982); *The Emergency English Workbook: Practical Reading and Writing Lessons for North American Students* (1980). Other publications include numerous newspaper and magazine articles as well as easy-to-read materials developed specifically for adult new readers. Ms. Lane has also produced and directed several films, slide-and-tape modules, and two videotape workshops, all on the subject of adult literacy and/or English for speakers of other languages.

Frank Charles Laubach (1884–1970)

Once called "Mr. Literacy" by *Time* magazine, Frank Laubach devoted most of his life to spreading literacy throughout the world. He first began developing his phonetically based methods for teaching reading, along with the "Each One Teach One" philosophy of using volunteer tutors, as a missionary in the Philippines during the 1930s. For the next 40 years, Dr. Laubach worked as a literacy crusader and consultant to governments, churches, and private organizations in 103 countries. In 1955 he founded Laubach Literacy International (LLI), which now supports a worldwide network of trained volunteers and has its own publishing company, the New Readers Press. The U.S. arm of LLI, Laubach Literacy Action (LLA), is the largest volunteer literacy organization in the country, employing some 50,000 volunteers in over 600 projects throughout the United States. The religious, philosophical, and psychological ideas behind the Laubach literacy program are portrayed in Dr. Laubach's 1970 book, *Forty Years with the Silent Billion: Adventures in Literacy,* which describes his experiences teaching people to read, developing materials, training tutors, and establishing literacy programs worldwide.

In addition to a doctorate from Columbia University, Dr. Laubach held honorary doctorates from several colleges and universities.

PUBLICATIONS: Frank Laubach was a prolific author whose works included books and articles on a variety of topics, including religious and educational subjects, sociology, history, and international affairs. He also coauthored over 200 primers for illiterate adults in 165 languages.

Helen Huguenor Lyman (1910–)

Helen Lyman, library educator, author, and researcher, began her long and distinguished career as a circulation assistant in the Buffalo (New York) Public Library in 1932. In 1943, she became head of the library's adult education department, and since then has made substantial contributions in the field of adult education and services in libraries. In 1952 she left the Buffalo Public Library to direct a national adult education survey for the American Library Association (ALA). Over the next several years she worked as a specialist in adult services for the Chicago Public Library, the Wisconsin Free Library Commission, and the Library Services Branch of the U.S. Department of Education. From 1967 to 1972, she was the director and principal investigator of the Library Materials in Service to the Adult New Reader research project at the University of Wisconsin–Madison. She has consulted with universities, libraries, and literacy providers throughout the United States, Canada, and Australia.

Dr. Lyman served as professor emeritus at the Library School at the University of Wisconsin from 1966 to 1978 and was a visiting professor and lecturer at library schools at a number of other universities, specializing in the areas of literacy and new readers. Since retiring from her professorship, she continues to work as a consultant, researcher, teacher, and writer.

Dr. Lyman's honors include the American Library Association's Joseph W. Lippincott Award for Distinguished Librarianship (1979), the Margaret E. Monroe Library Adult Services Award (1986), and appearances in *Who's Who of American Women, Contemporary Authors,* and the *ALA (American Library Association) Yearbook.*

PUBLICATIONS: Books include *Adult Education Activities in Public Libraries* (1954); *Library Materials in Service to the Adult New Reader* (1970, rev. 1974); *Reading and the Adult New Reader* (1976); *Literacy and the Nation's Libraries* (1977). She has also published pamphlets, reports, handbooks, and numerous articles and papers. Since 1977, Dr. Lyman has written the annual report on literacy and libraries for the *ALA Yearbook.*

Harold W. McGraw, Jr. (1918–   )

Harold McGraw, Chairman of the Board of McGraw-Hill book publishers, has in the last few years become the leading corporate spokesperson for literacy in the United States. Mr. McGraw, who has worked in the publishing industry for over 40 years, has made literacy a major focus since he retired as McGraw-Hill's chief executive officer in 1983. In that year he used his own funds to establish the Business Council for Effective Literacy (BCEL), a publicly supported foundation aimed at fostering greater corporate awareness of adult functional illiteracy and increasing business involvement in the literacy field. In addition to his work at BCEL, of which he is the president, Mr. McGraw travels extensively to speak to groups of business leaders about the need for corporate involvement in literacy efforts.

Mr. McGraw's many other civic activities include presiding over the Princeton University Press and being a vice chairman of the New York Public Library and a trustee of the Council for Aid to Education. He also established and chairs another foundation, the Business Press Educational Foundation. Mr. McGraw holds honorary doctorates from the City University of New York, Ohio University, and Princeton University.

Ruth S. Nickse (1940–)

Ruth Nickse has been involved in educational research and innovative program development, particularly in the areas of adult literacy and competency-based education, since the early 1970s. From 1973 to 1976, she directed the New York State External High School Diploma Program, in which she was responsible for designing, developing, implementing, and field testing one of the country's first external, competency-based high school diploma programs for adults. As an Educational Policy Fellow for the National Institute of Education (NIE), she developed major research agendas in competency-based education and testing. As a consultant, she has worked with local school districts, state departments of education, the NIE, and national educational laboratories in identifying adult competencies, designing and administering adult external diploma programs, and developing applied performance testing. She was a senior scholar and advisory member for the NIE-sponsored Adult Literacy Project and is a frequent presenter, workshop leader, and symposium coordinator at professional conferences.

In 1987, Dr. Nickse founded the Family Learning Center, a Boston University–based model program that uses college work-study participants to tutor high school dropouts and their children in an attempt to break the cycle of intergenerational illiteracy. In addition to directing the center, she teaches under-graduate and graduate courses in adult education and literacy at the university, where she is an associate professor. Dr. Nickse received her doctorate in educational psychology from Cornell University in 1972.

Among Dr. Nickse's honors are the Program Development Award (for the New York State External High School Diploma Program) from the Adult Competency Education Unit of the American Association of Adult and Continuing Education (1985); the U.S. Department of Education Award for recognition of adult literacy efforts; the National Association for Public Continuing Adult Education award for outstanding achievement in adult education (1975); and *Who's Who of American Women* (1973).

PUBLICATIONS: Books include *Competency-Based Education: Beyond Minimum Competency Testing* (ed. 1981); *Administrators Handbook: An Intergenerational Reading Project* (1985); chapter in *Survey and Guide to the Use of Microcomputers in Correctional Education* (1987). Other publications include numerous reports, monographs, Educational Resources Information Center (ERIC) reports, articles, and papers.

Elaine Shelton (1943–)

Elaine Shelton has been instrumental in the development and promotion of competency-based adult education (CBAE) programs in the United States. CBAE is based largely on the findings of the Adult Performance Level (APL) study, in which Ms. Shelton was an active participant. As a research associate with the APL Project, she wrote criterion-referenced test items used in the national survey of adult functional competency and created learning activities for the curriculum designed to teach toward APL objectives. In the mid-1970s, she developed and disseminated the APL Competency-Based High School Diploma Program for Adults; subsequently she managed the APL developer/demonstrator grant with the U.S. Department of Education's National Diffusion Network. From 1983 to 1985, Ms. Shelton served as a senior researcher and dissemination specialist for the National Institute of Education's Adult Literacy Project. She is a member of the national curriculum committee for "The American Ticket" series being produced by KCET-TV of Los Angeles for Project Literacy U.S., an advisor to the Business Council for Effective Literacy, and president of Shelton Associates, specializing in CBAE.

In 1987, Ms. Shelton was elected president of the American Association for Adult and Continuing Education (AAACE). She was named the Adult Educator of the Year by the Commission on Adult Basic Education of the AAACE in 1983 and received the Program Development Award of the Adult Competency Education unit of the AAACE in 1985.

PUBLICATIONS: Books include *The Adult Performance Level Competency-Based High School Diploma Program* (1978); *Managing Money* (for adult new readers, 1982); *Texas Adult Education Curriculum Guide* (1984). She has also published reports, articles in professional journals, bibliographies, and a chapter on competency-based adult education in *Materials and Methods in Adult and Continuing Education* (1987).

Stephen Joseph Steurer (1944–)

Stephen Steurer is the executive director of the Correctional Education Association (CEA), a post he has held since 1986. He has been involved in adult education, particularly in correctional education, since 1977, and has worked in reading research and instruction since 1973. He taught reading instruction for secondary schoolteachers; did research in the areas of reading evaluation and remediation for problem readers of all ages; and designed, developed, and evaluated a variety of reading programs and materials. One of his projects involved developing low readability driving manuals under a Department of Transportation grant in 1974–1975; in 1980 he wrote a manual and workbook for the New Readers Press *Wheels* series, which was used to teach adult education and high school students how to obtain a driver's license and buy and maintain a car.

Dr. Steurer received his doctorate in secondary education,

with an emphasis on reading, from the University of Maryland in 1976. In addition to his role as executive director of CEA, Dr. Steurer also serves as a correctional academic specialist to the Maryland State Department of Education and is an auditor for the Commission on Accreditation for Corrections. He writes and speaks frequently on working with adult illiterates and competency-based vocational education in correctional settings.

PUBLICATIONS: *Help Yourself to Health Workbook* (1983); *Wheels Teachers Manual* (1980) and *Wheels Student Workbook* (1980) (for New Readers Press); *Speak English! Functional American English for the Modern World,* with Mary Ann Corley (1980, reprinted in 1984); plus articles in professional journals and magazines.

Cora Wilson Stewart (1875–1958)

In 1911, Cora Wilson Stewart, the superintendent of public schools in Rowan County, Kentucky, opened the public schools to adults on moonlit nights. Some 1,200 adults, nearly all with no previous schooling, enrolled in the Moonlight Schools to learn basic language, history, civics, agriculture, and sanitation concepts from volunteer teachers. Mrs. Stewart edited a weekly newspaper, *The Rowan County School Messenger,* which was used in the classes in place of textbooks. Using short sentences and word repetitions for easy reading, it featured school and county news and represented one of the first efforts to develop instructional materials directed at adults. By 1912, the Moonlight Schools had spread to 12 counties and were serving 1,600 students. The schools served as inspiration for similar campaigns in South Carolina, Alabama, Oklahoma, Washington, Minnesota, New Hampshire, Georgia, Mississippi, Arkansas, New York, Pennsylvania, and other states.

In 1926, Cora Stewart was appointed to the National Illiteracy Crusade by President Calvin Coolidge. In 1929, President Herbert Hoover named her to direct the National Illiteracy Commission. She later chaired the illiteracy committee of the World Federation of Education Associations. Among her honors were the Clara Barton and Ella Flagg Young medals in 1930 and awards from *Pictorial Review* magazine (1924) and the General Federation of Women's Clubs.

PUBLICATIONS: *Moonlight Schools for the Emancipation of Adults* (1922), which discussed the *Rowan County Messenger* and its function in teaching adults; *County Life Readers,* two books written at a first- or second-grade level that dealt with problems of rural life (1915 and 1916); *Soldier's First Book* (1917), used by the army to teach illiterate soldiers; and *Mother's First Book* (1930).

Thomas Sticht*

Thomas Sticht has been actively involved in literacy research and innovative program development for many years, with a particular emphasis on literacy skills as they relate to the actual requirements of work. He has conducted extensive research on literacy and basic skills for the military, the National Aeronautics and Space Administration (NASA), and the Ford Foundation, and served as consultant to a variety of projects and organizations. In his work, Dr. Sticht applies principles of cognitive psychology and the ways in which people learn to a unique approach called functional context education. Functional context education seeks to impart literacy skills not in isolation but in the context of specialized, useful knowledge, usually employment-related. It builds on the knowledge already possessed by students to help them acquire not only literacy but knowledge and skills needed for real-world situations and employment. It also relies on two important elements—well-designed materials and high motivational level—that increase the ability of "mid-level literates" to learn from printed materials, even those written above the reader's supposed level.

Dr. Sticht currently heads Applied Behavioral and Cognitive Sciences, Inc., a San Diego–based research and program development company. In 1987, the Ford Foundation sponsored a series of workshops on functional context education developed by Dr. Sticht and presented around the country. Dr. Sticht, who earned his doctorate in experimental and cognitive psychology from the University of Arizona, recently participated in a two-year research project on the military's experience with teaching basic skills. The report of that project, *Cast-off Youth: Policy and Training Methods from the Military Experience,* was published in 1987.

PUBLICATIONS: Books include *Reading for Working: A Functional Literacy Anthology* (ed., 1975); *Auding and Reading: A Developmental Model* (coauthor, 1974); *Literacy and Vocational Competence* (1978); *Cast-off Youth: Policy and Training Methods from the Military Experience* (coauthor, 1987); *Functional Context Education: Workshop Research Notebook* (1987). He has also published numerous chapters in books, reports, papers, and articles.

*birthdate not available

Terilyn C. Turner (1946–)

Terilyn Turner is a leading proponent of using technology for teaching adults to read. Furthermore, she is an innovator who has put her theories into active and successful practice. Realizing that computers offered a way for people to learn "without having to learn to please a teacher," Dr. Turner designed and planned what is generally believed to be the first adult literacy computer program in the country—the Adult Basic Literacy Education (ABLE) project at Central Piedmont Community College in Charlotte, North Carolina. By the time ABLE became operative in 1983, Dr. Turner had moved to Minnesota, where she planned, designed, and now directs the Technology for Literacy Center (TLC) in St. Paul. Located in a shopping mall for easy access, TLC uses computers and volunteer tutors to teach reading skills to adults. The center also provides training to adult educators in colleges, public schools, and literacy programs on the use of technology and does research in the application of technology to addressing functional illiteracy.

A former teacher whose students ranged from kindergarten to graduate school, Dr. Turner received her doctorate from the University of North Carolina in 1977. In addition to directing TLC, she is involved in a number of other literacy activities, including chairing the Minnesota Adult Literacy Coalition, consulting to numerous projects around the country, and serving on the National Steering Committee for the Adult Literacy and Technology Project.

Peter A. Waite (1951–)

Peter Waite heads Laubach Literacy Action (LLA), which, with programs throughout the United States and 35,000 members, is the largest volunteer literacy program in the United States. Dr. Waite has been active in literacy efforts since 1979, when he became the executive director of Washington Literacy, Inc., in Seattle. He has been involved in alternative education programs for youth and adults, including programs for potential dropouts and youth in correctional settings, since 1973. His work in those programs involved a wide range of activities, including program development, implementation, and evaluation, staff training, administration, and teaching.

Dr. Waite received his doctorate in educational administration and leadership, public administration, from Seattle University in 1984. In addition to his work with LLA, he has been a speaker and presenter at a number of literacy conferences and workshops around the country.

PUBLICATIONS: *A Resource Guide to Cooperative Literacy Projects* (1981); *CHOICES: A Guide to Educational Alternatives* (1975); plus various articles and papers.

3

Facts and Data

THE INTENT OF THIS CHAPTER is to provide readers with a basis for evaluating the language and statistics that are popularly used to describe literacy/illiteracy in the United States, as well as to provide interesting background information in several related areas. It includes six sections:

Definitions   This section presents a number of different viewpoints on what constitutes literacy/illiteracy in the present-day United States.

Some Attempts at Measuring   This section gives an overview of recent attempts to quantify levels of literacy in the adult population.

How Much and What Do Adults Read?   This section gives an overview of how much adults read and the types of materials they read on a day-to-day basis.

A Readability Comparison   This section compares the "readability" scores of passages in some common adult reading materials, using various popular indexes.

Adult Education Legislation   This section presents an overview of the Adult Education Act and related federal legislation.

National Student Proclamations   This section contains a set of proclamations developed by delegates to the first National Adult Literacy Congress, held in September 1987 in Philadelphia.

Definitions

Until relatively recently, *literacy* was defined according to such easily quantifiable standards as the ability to sign one's name or the number of grades completed in school. As society has grown more complex, however, so have the requirements for and the definitions of literacy. As we approach the last decade of the twentieth century, few people accept absolute standards of literacy. In fact, there is nothing resembling a consensus on what constitutes literacy or illiteracy; there is not even a consensus on what terms are being defined: *literacy/illiteracy, functional literacy, functional competency,* and *adult competency* are but some of the terms being used.

The difficulties in defining literacy have been discussed at length elsewhere; this book will not attempt to continue that discussion. Instead, it presents a sampling of the many definitions that have been offered, with the authors' own selections of terms. Readers who wish to pursue the thorny pathway of definition further are referred to the bibliography in Chapter 5.

> A person is literate who can with understanding both read and write a short, simple statement on his everyday life (UNESCO 1951 [cited in Hunter and Harman, 13]).

> [Literacy is] the possession by an individual of the essential knowledge and skills which enable him or her to engage in all those activities required for effective functioning in his or her group and community and whose attainments in reading, writing, and arithmetic make it possible for him or her to continue to use these skills toward his or her own and the community's development (UNESCO 1962 [cited in Hunter and Harman, 14]).[1]

> [Functional literacy is] the ability to read, write and compute with the functional competence needed for meeting the requirements of adult living. (NACAE 1986, 11).

> Within the general term *literacy,* we suggest the following distinctions:
>
> 1. *Conventional literacy*: the ability to read, write, and comprehend texts on familiar subjects and to understand whatever signs, labels, instructions, and directions are necessary to get along within one's environment.
> 2. *Functional literacy*: the possession of skills *perceived as necessary by particular persons and groups* to fulfill their

own self-determined objectives as family and community members, citizens, consumers, job-holders, and members of social, religious, or other associations of their choosing. This includes the ability to obtain information they want and to use that information for their own and others' well-being, to satisfy the requirements *they set for themselves* as being important for their own lives; the ability to deal positively with demands made on them by society; and the ability to solve the problems they face in their daily lives (Hunter and Harman 1979, 7–8).

Functional illiteracy . . . is perhaps best defined as the inability to read, write or compute well enough to accomplish the kinds of basic and pervasive tasks necessary for everyday adult living (Lerche 1985, 1).

Adult competency is a function of both individual capabilities and societal requirements. . . . A person is functionally competent only to the extent that he or she can meet the requirements which are extant at a given point in time. If the requirements change and the individual does not adapt by either acquiring more or different knowledges and skills, then that person becomes less competent. Functional competence is a dynamic process, rather than a static state (Northcutt 1975, 2).

[Literacy is the ability to use] printed and written information to function in society, to achieve one's goals, and to develop one's knowledge and potential (Kirsch and Jungeblut 1986, 3–4).

[Literacy includes] not only the ability to literally decipher a simple written passage, but other skills as well: the ability to analyze and summarize, for example, and the ability to interpret passages inferentially as well as literally (ECS 1983, 17).

More than a set of skills, literacy is a value. . . . Literacy is not just a technical ability: it is a consciousness that must be internalized before an individual can be available for instruction (Harman 1987, 13).

Literacy is not simply reading, or reading plus writing, but an ability to use print for personal and social ends. It is a functional skill in that it requires the application of various skills in common, everyday situations. In this sense, the phrase 'functional literacy' is redundant, in that literacy, by definition, is a functional ability. Literacy is also a continuum of skills, not an all-or-none ability. One can define arbitrary levels of performance for designating discrete literate or illiterate categories . . . but this obscures the true literacy issue, which is what people can do and how these abilities relate to particular social needs (Venezky, Kaestle, and Sum 1987, 5).

Some Attempts at Measuring

As the first section of this chapter indicates, a large part of the problem with literacy statistics is a lack of consensus on what is being measured. This fact alone guarantees that there will be no consensus on the statistics themselves. Terminology is a large part of the problem—just as there is no universally accepted definition for *literacy,* there is also no firm agreement on the definitions for such critical terms as *adult* and *success.*

Therefore, to understand what the various measurements mean, one must first have some knowledge of what is being measured. A detailed analysis of the current statistics on adult literacy is far outside the scope of this book.[2] Instead, this section presents an overview of some of the more well known attempts to measure literacy levels in the United States, in order to allow readers to better consider the sources of the more popularly used statistics.

The sources discussed here are the U.S. Census Bureau, the Adult Performance Level (APL) Project, and the National Assessment of Educational Progress (NAEP).[3]

Census Bureau Statistics

From 1840 until 1930, the U.S. Census Bureau measured literacy rates by asking individuals whether they could read and write. Since 1940, the bureau has collected data on the basis of grade completion. The Census Bureau does periodically collect literacy data, using a conventional definition of literacy—that is, possession of simple reading and writing skills. As noted by Lee Soltow and Edward Stevens in *The Rise of Literacy and the Common School in the United States,* census data, although limited by definition, does the following: (1) establishes a minimum standard of literacy; (2) allows comparisons between occupational, ethnic, demographic, and geographic groups; and (3) offers a comprehensive, broad picture over an extended period (Soltow and Stevens 1982, 5–6). Census statistics may also be used to correlate educational levels with employment, ethnic background, geographical area, etc., and as such serve as the basis for a wide variety of statistical analyses and models.

Recent Census Bureau Statistics

In a 1979 survey, persons 14 and over with less than a sixth-grade education were counted as illiterate if they said that they could not read and write English at all or that they could not read and write a language other than English that they spoke at home. Based on a sample of fewer than 2,500 households, the Census Bureau estimated that 0.6 percent of the population could not read and write. According to the survey, the percentage of illiterates was less for younger than for older population groups; it was also generally less for white than for black groups.

Based on 1980 grade completion data, the Census Bureau estimated a 0.5 percent adult illiteracy rate for that year, a figure that represents approximately 0.9 million persons aged 14 and over. Overall, census figures show a steady decline in illiteracy rates from 1870 to 1980, as shown in Table 1.

TABLE 1

Percentage of the American Population Illiterate, 1870 to 1980

YEAR	PERCENT
1980	0.5
1969	1.0
1959	2.2
1952	2.5
1947	2.7
1930	4.3
1920	6.0
1910	7.7
1900	10.7
1890	13.3
1880	17.0
1870	20.0

Source: Irwin (1986), 4.

The English Language Proficiency Study

In the fall of 1982, the U.S. Bureau of the Census conducted a survey under contract to the Department of Education. The original aim of the survey, called the English Language Proficiency

Study, was to determine the number of English–language deficient children living in homes of non-English background. The majority of the 15,000 survey participants were children between the ages of 5 and 14 who took age-specific oral and written tests of English proficiency (children aged 5 and 6 took oral tests only).

At the request of the Department of Education, a test was added and administered to non–native-born adults. The test objective was to determine whether the adults had the English skills needed to participate in social service programs. Accordingly, nearly all of the 36 multiple-choice questions related in some way to social services. For example, in the first set of problems participants were to choose the answer that best matched the underlined word or phrase in a statement such as "Persons may receive benefits if they are *eligible*" or "This is to notify you that your application for assistance has been *denied*." In the second set, they were to choose the best answers to questions such as "What should you do if you do not understand the questions on the application form?" (U.S. Bureau of the Census 1982, 4, 6).

For control purposes, a group of native English-speaking adults also took the test, for a total of 3,400 adults. The test results for the entire adult group, which by its very nature was not a representative cross-section of U.S. adults, became the basis for an analysis conducted by the Department of Education in 1986. That study developed a model that sought to correlate passage or failure of the test with answers to standard Census Bureau questions. The figures thus gained were extrapolated to arrive at a "functional illiteracy rate" for the entire population—about 13 percent of adults over age 20.

It should be noted that the Census Bureau simply administered the survey and compiled the results; it did not carry out the analysis. In 1987, the (unanalyzed) data collected through the survey was recompiled into a computer-readable data file, which is available on tape from the Census Bureau for a minimal cost (see Chapter 6).

A summary of the Department of Education analysis is reprinted below.

Update On Adult Illiteracy

The Source

The English Language Proficiency Survey was commissioned by the U.S. Department of Education and conducted by the Bureau of the Census in the Fall of 1982. At that time, simple written tests of English comprehension were administered in the home to a national sample of 3,400 adults, ages 20 and over.

Major Findings

Between 17 and 21 million U.S. adults are illiterate, for an overall rate of nearly 13 percent. In contrast to traditional estimates of illiteracy based on completion of fewer than six years of school, this new study shows that illiterate adults are now much more likely to be located in our major cities, and most are under the age of 50. Immigration and reliance on a non-English language are also major factors; nearly half of all adults using a non-English language at home failed the test of English proficiency. More specifically,

Of all adults classified as illiterate

- ☐ 41 percent live in central cities of metropolitan areas, compared to just 8 percent in rural areas
- ☐ 56 percent are under the age of 50
- ☐ 37 percent speak a non-English language at home

Among native English speakers classified as illiterate

- ☐ 70 percent did not finish high school
- ☐ 42 percent had no earnings in the previous year (1981)
- ☐ 35 percent are in their twenties and thirties

Among illiterate adults who use a non-English language

- ☐ 82 percent were born outside the United States
- ☐ 42 percent live in neighborhoods where exclusive reliance on English is the exception rather than the rule

☐ 21 percent had entered the United States within the previous six years

☐ About 14 percent are probably literate in their non-English language (judging from their reported education)

The Test and the Definition of Illiteracy

The test employed is called the Measure of Adult English Proficiency (MAEP). The written portion of MAEP consists of 26 questions which test the individual's ability to identify key words and phrases and match these with one of four fixed-choice alternatives. Based on an analysis of the number of questions answered correctly out of 26, a literacy cutoff of 20 was selected as providing the best discrimination between high and low risk groups. Specifically, among native English speakers, less than 1 percent of those completing some college scored below 20, in contrast to a failure rate of more than 50 percent for those with fewer than 6 years of school.

How the Test Results Compare with Traditional Estimates Based on Fewer than Six Years of School

Our estimate of illiteracy is about three-and-a-half times the number of U.S. adults with fewer than 6 years of school—18.7 versus 5.2 million. More important, however, are the compositional differences between the two approaches to estimating illiteracy, especially with respect to age. For example, among native English-speaking adults, only 0.6 percent of those in their twenties and thirties completed fewer than six years of school, compared with 3.9 percent for those age 40 and over. This suggests a six-to-one differential in illiteracy rates between the two age groups, but based on direct testing, we estimate there is less than a three-to-one difference: adults under age 40 have an observed rate of 5.2 percent, compared with 14.1 percent for those 40 and over. This means that the illiteracy rate for the younger group is eight-and-a-half times greater than it should be if completion of six or more years of school was a guarantee of literacy.

Accuracy of These Estimates

The standard error of our point estimate (18.7 million) is about 1 million. Thus, we can be quite confident (95 chances out of a 100)

that the true figure is in the range of 17 to 21 million. The standard of literacy, however, has a far greater potential impact on our estimates than sampling error. Selecting 21 rather than 20 items correct as our standard of literacy adds about 3 million to the total estimate. We do not believe that lower estimates are supportable, but higher estimates can readily be obtained by setting more exacting standards of literacy. However, within the limitations of the MAEP test, we believe our approach is preferable, since it maximizes the discrimination between high and low risk groups.

The Adult Performance Level (APL) Study

The Adult Performance Level (APL) study was commissioned by the Department of Education in 1971 and carried out over a period of several years by a team at the University of Texas at Austin. Its purpose was to "specify the competencies which are functional to economic and educational success in today's society and to develop devices for assessing those competencies of the adult population of the United States" (Northcutt 1975, 1). Although it was completed over a decade ago, the APL study serves as the basis of many of the statistics that are popularly used today. The competencies identified by the study have been used to develop curricula for competency-based education, which has become increasingly popular in formal adult education programs.

The APL Project team began by identifying a set of five general knowledge areas and four sets of primary skills that comprised the "basic requirements for adult living." The knowledge areas were consumer economics, occupational knowledge, community resources, health, and government and law. The primary skills were communication, which included reading, writing, speaking, and listening; computation; problem solving; and interpersonal relations. Functional competency was then described as the application of primary skills to knowledge areas, as shown in Figure 1.

The performance requirements were used to arrive at a set of goals and objectives for each general knowledge area. Mastery of the objectives, based on performance of a series of situation-specific requirements called tasks, was considered to be an indication of competency. For example, the goal for the area of occupational knowledge was "to develop a level of occupational knowledge which will enable adults to secure employment in accordance with their individual needs and interests." A sample objective in this area was "to identify sources of information (e.g. radio broadcasts, newspapers, etc.) which may lead to employment" (Northcutt 1975, A2).

FIGURE 1

APL Model of Functional Competency

	Consumer Economics	Occupational Knowledge	Health	Community Resources	Government & Law
Reading	Reading a newspaper grocery ad	Reading a newspaper help-wanted ad	Reading and interpreting a health insurance policy	Reading a movie schedule	Reading a pamphlet on an individual rights after arrest
Writing	Writing a grocery list				
Speaking, Listening	Listening to an advertisement on the radio		Performance Requirements		
Computation	Computing the unit price of a grocery item				
Problem-Solving	Determining the best stores to shop in				

Levels of Competency

On the assumption that more competent adults would be more successful, the team created an "index of success" that was a composite of income, level of education, and occupational status. The index was used to establish three levels of functional competency. These were in turn used to develop "competency profiles," which are associated with different levels of adult success as measured by income, education, and job status:

APL 1 consists of adults who are functionally incompetent (or who function with difficulty). This level is associated with:

1. inadequate income of poverty level or less;
2. inadequate education of eight years or fewer of schooling; and
3. unemployment or employment in a low-status occupation.

APL 2 consists of adults who are functionally competent (or minimally competent). This level is associated with:

1. income over poverty level but not discretionary income;
2. educational level of nine to eleven years of schooling; and
3. employment in a mid-level-status occupation (i.e., blue-collar).

APL 3 consists of adults who are proficient. This level is associated with:

1. high levels of income or varying amounts of discretionary income;
2. high levels of education, high school completion or more; and
3. employment in a high-status occupation (i.e., white-collar or professional) (Northcutt 1975, 5).

Using test data to "predict" adults' success level on the above scale, the APL study conducted a national survey of 7,500 adults. The results, published in 1975, indicated that 20 percent of the sample were functionally incompetent, 34 percent were marginally competent or "just getting by," and 46 percent were fully competent or proficient. The study found, among other things, that the general knowledge area of greatest difficulty was consumer economics, and that a greater proportion of persons were unable to perform basic computations than other skills.

The competency levels were further broken down by demographic groups, as shown in Table 2.

TABLE 2

Adult Competency Levels by Demographic Groupings
(estimated percent of population)

DEMOGRAPHIC VARIABLE	APL COMPETENCY LEVEL		
	1	2	3
Education			
0–3 years	85	10	6
4–5	84	16	0
6–7	49	37	14
8–11	18	55	27
High school completed	11	37	52
Some college	9	27	64
College graduate plus	2	17	80
Family Income			
under $5,000	40	39	21
$5,000–$6,999	20	44	36
$7,000–$9,999	24	39	37
$10,000–$14,999	14	34	52
$15,000 plus	8	26	66
Job Status			
Unskilled	30	38	32
Semiskilled	29	42	29
Skilled	24	33	43
Clerical-Sales	8	38	54
Professional-Managerial	11	28	61
Age			
18–29	16	35	49
30–39	11	29	60
40–49	19	32	49
50–59	28	37	35
60–65	35	40	24
Sex			
Male	17	31	52
Female	23	35	42
Ethnicity			
White	16	34	50
Black	44	39	17
Spanish-surname	56	26	18
Other	26	41	33
Occupational Status			
Employed	15	28	57
Unemployed	36	30	34
Housewives	27	38	35
Number in Household			
1 person	21	23	56
2–3	20	35	45
4–5	19	31	50
6–7	21	33	46
8 plus	43	22	35

Continued on next page

TABLE 2—*Continued*

**Adult Competency Levels by Demographic Groupings
(estimated percent of population)**

DEMOGRAPHIC VARIABLE	APL COMPETENCY LEVEL		
	1	2	3
Region			
Northeast	16	36	48
North Central	15	42	43
South	25	37	38
West	15	35	50
Metropolitan Areas			
1 million plus	21	39	40
under 1 million	15	38	47
Suburb	21	32	47
Urban	14	29	57

Source: Northcutt (1975), 7–8.

In 1975, the APL study estimated the number of functionally incompetent adults to be 23 million, with 39 million being marginally competent and 53 million being proficient. If the APL percentages are applied to recent census figures, they indicate 29 million functionally incompetent adults, 49 million marginally competent adults, and 67 million proficient adults aged 18 to 64 (out of a total of 145 million) as of 1983 (Irwin 1986, 6). The first figure, incidentally, corresponds with the 1980 census count of adults with a less than eighth-grade education, 24.4 million.

Based on the assumption that "marginal competence" is insufficient for our technologically complex society, adults in the first two levels are sometimes grouped together. This gives a figure of 54 percent, or more than 70 million adults, who are not functioning at a "proficient" level and who on that basis are judged to be "functionally illiterate."

Criticisms of the APL

The APL study generated considerable controversy, primarily because of the confusion between "success" skills and "survival" skills, and the fact that the team's definition of success was determined by a relatively limited set of values. Certainly many of the persons classified as illiterate or functionally illiterate on the basis of APL criteria are capable of basic reading, writing, and computation; further, many of them are probably quite successful by their own definitions of success.

Additionally, the APL study itself is over ten years old; it may be inaccurate to presume that the percentages can be applied to recent population figures to arrive at current competency rates. Further, the study found the highest rates of functional incompetency in the highest age groups (50 to 65 years). These people are now 60 to 75 years old. Among younger adults the rates of functional incompetency are considerably lower, as indicated by the APL study itself and the 1985 National Assessment of Educational Progress (NAEP) study (see below). Attempts to gain federal funding for an updated study have thus far been unsuccessful.

For more about the APL study, see *Adult Functional Competency: A Summary* (1975), and *Final Report: The Adult Performance Level Study* (1977), both published by the University of Texas at Austin; and *APL Revisited: Its Uses and Adaptations in States,* published by the National Institute of Education in 1980.

The National Assessment of Educational Progress (NAEP)—Young Adult Study

In 1985, the National Assessment of Educational Progress (NAEP) undertook to assess the literacy skills of young adults in the United States. Rather than attempting to measure conventional or functional literacy, the study was designed to determine young adults' ability to *process* printed and written information, including tables, charts, graphs, maps, and other types of material as well as text.

The assessment involved a nationally representative sample of approximately 3,600 adults between the ages of 21 and 25; some 40,000 households in the 48 contiguous states were contacted to locate the participants. Participants were interviewed individually, with each interview lasting about 90 minutes. A third of each interview was used to obtain background information such as current reading and writing activities, occupational status and aspirations, educational and early language experiences, and home characteristics. The remaining time was used to measure proficiencies on literacy tasks that simulated those encountered in various adult settings. The tasks were designed to measure three distinct types of literacy skills:

prose literacy the knowledge and skills needed to understand and use information from texts that include editorials, news stories, poems, and the like;

document literacy the knowledge and skills required to locate and use information contained in job applications or payroll forms, bus schedules, maps, tables, indexes, and so forth; and,

quantitative literacy the knowledge and skills needed to apply arithmetic operations, either alone or sequentially, that are embedded in printed materials, such as balancing a checkbook, figuring out a tip, completing an order form, or determining the amount of interest from a loan advertisement (Kirsch and Jungeblut 1986, 4).

The tasks in each group were rated according to levels of difficulty on "proficiency scales" extending from 0 to 500. Respondents also completed a representative set of multiple-choice exercises from the NAEP reading scale used to evaluate reading skills among in-school populations, for a total of four scales.

Prose Literacy

The easiest tasks in the area of prose literacy included locating a single piece of information from a short newspaper article (level 210) and writing a simple description of a job one would like to have (level 199). The most difficult tasks required using text information to compare two different types of employee fringe benefits (level 371) and describing the theme of a short poem (level 387). Table 3 shows the prose task levels and the percentages of participants in various educational and racial/ethnic groups who were able to successfully complete tasks at each level.

Document Literacy

The easiest document literacy tasks included locating the expiration date on a driver's license (level 160) and signing one's name on a social security card (level 110), while several of the most difficult tasks involved interpreting a bus schedule (average level 350). Table 4 shows the document task levels and the percentages of participants in various educational and racial/ethnic groups who were able to successfully complete tasks at each level.

TABLE 3

**Percentages of People and Selected Tasks at or above
Successive Points on the Prose Scale[1]**

	SELECTED TASKS AT DECREASING LEVELS OF DIFFICULTY[2]	SELECTED POINTS ON THE SCALE	TOTAL
		500	
397	Identify appropriate Information in lengthy newspaper column		
387	Generate unfamiliar theme from short poem		
		375	8.8 (0.7)
371	Orally interpret distinctions between two types of employee benefits		
361	Select inappropriate title based on interpretation of news article		
		350	21.1 (1.1)
340	State in writing argument made in lengthy newspaper column		
339	Orally interpret a lengthy feature story in newspaper		
		325	37.1 (1.6)
313	Locate information in a news article		
		300	56.4 (1.5)
281	Locate information on a page of text in an almanac (3-feature)		
279	Interpret instructions from an appliance warranty		
278	Generate familiar theme of poem		
277	Write letter to state that an error has been made in billing		
		275	71.5 (1.4)
262	Locate Information in sports article (2-feature)		
		250	82.7 (1.2)
		225	90.8 (0.7)
210	Locate information in sports article (1-feature)		
199	Write about a job one would like		
		200	96.1 (0.5)
		175	98.5 (0.2)
		150	99.7 (0.1)
		0	

Source: Kirsch and Jungeblut (1986), 17. Reprinted with permission of Educational Testing Service.

[1]Numbers in parentheses are estimated standard errors.

[2]Number indicating difficulty level designates that point on the scale at which individuals with that level of proficiency have an 80 percent probability of responding correctly.

[3]High school diploma and/or some postsecondary experience.

TABLE 3—*Continued*

**Percentages of People and Selected Tasks at or above
Successive Points on the Prose Scale[1]**

RACE/ETHNICITY			LEVELS OF EDUCATION			
White	Black	Hispanic	0-8 Years	9-12 Years	H.S. Diploma and/or More[3]	2- or 4-Yr. Deg. or More
10.8 (0.9)	0.7 (0.3)	3.3 (1.1)	0.0 (0.0)	1.8 (1.1)	3.2 (0.8)	19.4 (1.5)
24.9 (1.3)	3.1 (0.6)	12.0 (3.2)	0.0 (0.0)	3.8 (1.5)	12.2 (1.3)	40.3 (2.0)
42.6 (1.7)	10.5 (1.6)	23.5 (3.4)	0.0 (0.0)	9.7 (1.6)	26.6 (1.8)	62.9 (1.7)
63.2 (1.4)	23.7 (1.6)	41.1 (4.1)	12.2 (9.5)	25.1 (2.8)	48.4 (1.7)	80.5 (1.3)
78.0 (1.3)	39.9 (1.9)	57.4 (3.2)	23.4 (8.7)	41.4 (2.7)	66.6 (1.4)	91.4 (1.0)
88.0 (1.0)	57.5 (2.7)	72.1 (2.6)	27.0 (8.3)	58.7 (3.4)	81.4 (1.3)	96.1 (0.5)
94.6 (0.6)	73.6 (2.3)	80.8 (2.3)	53.7 (7.7)	73.0 (2.1)	91.2 (0.9)	98.8 (0.3)
98.0 (0.4)	86.2 (1.5)	93.8 (1.5)	71.2 (8.7)	88.1 (1.9)	96.7 (0.6)	99.6 (0.2)
99.4 (0.2)	94.1 (0.9)	96.6 (1.2)	91.8 (3.1)	93.5 (1.1)	99.0 (0.2)	99.9 (0.1)
100.0 (0.0)	97.7 (0.5)	99.8 (0.2)	97.1 (1.4)	98.7 (0.4)	99.7 (0.1)	100.0 (0.0)

TABLE 4

Percentages of People and Selected Tasks at or above
Successive Points on the Document Scale[1]

SELECTED TASKS AT DECREASING LEVELS OF DIFFICULTY[2]		SELECTED POINTS ON THE SCALE	TOTAL
		500	
		375	8.8 (0.8)
365	Use bus schedule to select appropriate bus for given departures & arrivals		
343		350	20.2 (1.3)
334			
320	Use sandpaper chart to locate appropriate grade given specifications	325	37.6 (1.6)
300	Follow directions to travel from one location to another using a map	300	57.2 (1.7)
294	Identify information from graph depicting source of energy and year		
278	Use index from an almanac		
		275	73.1 (1.2)
262	Locate eligibility from table of employee benefits		
257	Locate gross pay-to-date on pay stub		
255	Complete a check given information on a bill		
253	Complete an address on order form		
249	Locate intersection on street map	250	83.8 (1.0)
221	Enter date on a deposit slip	225	91.0 (0.8)
219	Identify cost of theatre trip from notice		
211	Match items on shopping list to coupons		
196	Enter personal information on job application	200	95.5 (0.5)
192	Locate movie in TV listing in newspaper		
181	Enter caller's number on phone message form		
		175	98.4 (0.3)
169	Locate time of meeting on a form		
160	Locate expiration date on driver's license		
		150	99.7 (0.1)
110	Sign your name		
		0	

Source: Kirsch and Jungeblut (1986), 29. Reprinted with permission of Educational Testing Service.

[1]Numbers in parentheses are estimated standard errors.

[2]Number indicating difficulty level designates that point on the scale at which individuals with that level of proficiency have an 80 percent probability of responding correctly.

[3]High school diploma and/or some postsecondary experience.

TABLE 4—*Continued*

Percentages of People and Selected Tasks at or above Successive Points on the Document Scale[1]

RACE/ETHNICITY			LEVELS OF EDUCATION			
White	Black	Hispanic	0-8 Years	9-12 Years	H.S. Diploma and/or More[3]	2- or 4-Yr. Deg. or More
10.5 (1.0)	0.9 (0.4)	3.2 (1.6)	0.0 (0.0)	0.0 (0.0)	2.6 (0.5)	20.7 (1.4)
24.3 (1.6)	2.5 (0.5)	6.7 (2.0)	0.7 (0.7)	0.8 (0.5)	10.9 (1.3)	40.7 (1.9)
44.0 (1.8)	9.0 (1.1)	20.8 (3.1)	0.7 (0.7)	7.5 (1.4)	28.0 (1.7)	63.2 (1.8)
65.4 (1.7)	19.8 (1.5)	37.0 (4.1)	11.0 (9.6)	22.0 (2.9)	50.2 (2.1)	81.8 (1.5)
80.8 (1.1)	38.7 (2.6)	54.7 (3.8)	21.1 (12.4)	39.5 (3.6)	70.6 (1.5)	91.4 (1.0)
89.9 (0.8)	55.5 (2.7)	69.0 (3.4)	31.5 (10.7)	59.1 (3.9)	83.4 (1.2)	96.0 (0.7)
95.0 (0.7)	71.0 (2.2)	84.4 (1.6)	47.3 (9.5)	72.0 (3.3)	91.8 (0.8)	98.9 (0.3)
97.9 (0.5)	82.3 (1.7)	91.5 (1.2)	61.8 (7.7)	84.0 (2.7)	96.9 (0.5)	99.4 (0.2)
99.3 (0.3)	93.2 (1.2)	96.5 (0.7)	75.7 (6.3)	94.2 (1.2)	99.2 (0.2)	99.9 (0.0)
99.9 (0.1)	98.6 (0.4)	99.1 (0.3)	96.7 (2.7)	98.8 (0.3)	99.8 (0.1)	100.0 (0.0)

Quantitative Literacy

In the quantitative literacy category, the lowest-level tasks included totalling two entries on a bank deposit slip (level 233). Tasks at the highest level of difficulty included filling out an order form, calculating the cost of several items, and totalling the cost (level 371); and determining the least costly product in a group of products by using unit pricing information (level 376). Table 5 shows the quantitative task levels and the percentages of participants in various educational and racial/ethnic groups who were able to successfully complete tasks at each level.

Study Findings

Overall, the study found that the overwhelming majority of young adults performed adequately at the lower levels of each of the proficiency scales, and more than half performed within the middle ranges. At the higher levels, however, relatively few participants were able to successfully complete the assigned tasks. About 2 percent of those selected had such limited skills that they were not asked to perform the simulation tasks; about half of this group did not speak English. Those who did speak English responded to a set of oral language tasks that were also administered to a random sample of participants who completed the simulation tasks. The oral language–only group performed significantly below the simulation task subsample, indicating that young adults with limited literacy proficiency also demonstrate limited oral language skills.

The study found strong correlations between proficiency and educational levels; fewer young adults with less than a high school education were able to perform at the moderate and high levels. Differences between ethnic groups appeared at each level of education, with black young adults performing significantly below white participants, and Hispanic young adults performing about midway between the other two groups. Home-support factors, such as parents' education and access to literacy materials, were also found to be related to educational level and to reported literacy practices.

Study Conclusions

The study indicates that nearly all young adults are literate by the standard of a century ago—the ability to sign one's name.

About 95 percent are literate at the standard set by the military nearly 50 years ago; that is, they can read at or above the level of the average fourth grader. Eighty percent can read as well as or better than the average eighth grader, and over 60 percent can read at or above the eleventh-grade level.

The implications of the NAEP study go well beyond these outdated measures, however. As authors Kirsch and Jungeblut conclude, it is questionable "whether such simplistic standards adequately capture the broad and complex nature of literacy tasks encountered in today's society" (Kirsch and Jungeblut, 1986, 63). The NAEP study represents a serious attempt to "[provide] a means for understanding the various types and levels of literacy attained by young adults. The result is a more accurate representation not only of the complex information-processing demands found within a pluralistic society, but also of the range of skills and strategies that individuals demonstrate" (Kirsch and Jungeblut, 1986, 63–64). On these more complex levels, the study indicates a disturbing inability among young adults to use information effectively.

Further information about and analyses of the NAEP study may be found in *Literacy: Profiles of America's Young Adults* (1986), *Literacy: Profiles of America's Young Adults: Final Report* (1986), and *The Subtle Danger: Reflections on the Literacy Abilities of America's Young Adults* (1987), all published by the Educational Testing Service.

How Much and What Do Adults Read?

In considering literacy as it relates to people's everyday lives, it is helpful to know what, how much, and why adults read on a day-to-day basis, in order to place literacy activities in a context of real-life situations.

The information in this section is derived from reports of three studies on the reading habits of adults:

1. A survey conducted by the Educational Testing Service (ETS) from April to November of 1971. The survey of 5,067 adults over age 16 aimed to determine what was being read, by whom, for how long, and for

TABLE 5

**Percentages of People and Selected Tasks at or above
Successive Points on the Quantitative Scale[1]**

	SELECTED TASKS AT DECREASING LEVELS OF DIFFICULTY[2]	SELECTED POINTS ON THE SCALE	TOTAL
		500	
489	Determine amount of interest charges from loan ad		
376	Estimate cost using grocery unit-price labels	375	9.5 (0.9)
371	Calculate & total costs based on item costs from catalogue		
356	Determine tip given percentage of bill	350	22.5 (1.4)
340	Plan travel arrangements for meeting using flight schedule		
337	Determine correct change using menu		
		325	37.8 (1.6)
		300	56.0 (1.4)
293			
289	Enter & calculate checkbook balance		
281			
281		275	72.2 (1.1)
		250	84.7 (1.0)
233	Total bank deposit entry		
		225	92.4 (0.6)
		200	96.4 (0.4)
		175	98.6 (0.2)
		150	99.6 (0.1)
		0	

Source: Kirsch and Jungeblut (1986), 37. Reprinted with permission of Educational Testing Service.

[1]Numbers in parentheses are estimated standard errors.

[2]Number indicating difficulty level designates that point on the scale at which individuals with that level of proficiency have an 80 percent probability of responding correctly.

[3]High school diploma and/or some postsecondary experience.

TABLE 5—*Continued*

**Percentages of People and Selected Tasks at or above
Successive Points on the Quantitative Scale[1]**

RACE/ETHNICITY			LEVELS OF EDUCATION			
White	Black	Hispanic	0-8 Years	9-12 Years	H.S. Diploma and/or More[3]	2- or 4-Yr. Deg. or More
11.5 (1.0)	0.8 (0.4)	3.8 (1.7)	0.0 (0.0)	0.4 (0.4)	4.5 (0.7)	20.0 (1.7)
27.2 (1.7)	2.4 (0.8)	11.3 (2.7)	4.4 (4.0)	2.3 (0.8)	13.4 (1.3)	42.9 (2.3)
44.4 (1.7)	8.3 (1.6)	19.9 (3.5)	4.4 (4.0)	9.5 (1.6)	29.7 (2.0)	60.7 (2.1)
63.3 (1.5)	22.0 (2.1)	36.9 (4.4)	8.5 (4.5)	20.9 (2.7)	49.4 (1.9)	79.8 (1.6)
78.8 (1.1)	39.3 (1.9)	57.9 (3.8)	28.4 (7.6)	38.8 (2.7)	68.8 (1.4)	91.0 (1.2)
89.4 (0.9)	60.4 (2.5)	74.6 (3.0)	48.2 (12.3)	61.5 (3.2)	83.0 (1.1)	97.4 (0.7)
95.5 (0.6)	75.4 (1.5)	87.3 (1.8)	69.4 (8.8)	74.0 (2.3)	93.1 (0.7)	99.5 (0.2)
98.0 (0.4)	87.4 (1.5)	93.1 (1.3)	81.5 (5.9)	85.9 (2.0)	97.2 (0.5)	99.8 (0.1)
99.2 (0.2)	94.8 (0.9)	97.7 (0.6)	91.5 (2.9)	94.3 (1.2)	99.0 (0.2)	99.9 (0.0)
99.8 (0.1)	98.3 (0.5)	99.6 (0.3)	96.0 (2.1)	98.3 (0.6)	99.9 (0.1)	100.0 (0.0)

what reason, as well as how reading fit into people's daily activities. The results of the study were reported by Amil Sharon in *Reading Research Quarterly* in 1973.

2. A smaller but more recent study conducted for the International Reading Association (IRA) and reported by John Guthrie and Mary Seifert in the March 1983 issue of *Journal of Reading*. This study involved 109 adults selected at random from a community of 6,000. Results for this study were broken down by occupational group and by sex.

3. The National Assessment of Education Progress (NAEP) 1985 study of literacy profiles of young adults, which gathered information on reading activities in the course of interviews with study participants. Results were broken down by the participant's educational level, by parental education level, and by race.

How Much Do Adults Read?

All three surveys indicated that "reading is an ubiquitous activity of American adults" (Sharon 1973–1974, 150). The ETS study found that adults read an average of 106 minutes a day, while the IRA study found a median reading time of 157 minutes per day (the NAEP study did not break down reading activities by time spent). Much of the reading was done in the course of daily activities such as working, shopping, and recreation. Most of the time was spent reading newspapers, magazines, books, and job-related material, but time spent reading items such as labels and traffic and street signs was also included.

The reported average and median times for both the ETS and IRA studies represent considerable variation in the actual amount of reading done by individuals. In the ETS study, reading time per day ranged from eight hours or more (6 percent) to less than five minutes (slightly more than 6 percent). The median times reported in the IRA study ranged from a high of almost four hours for those in professional and managerial occupations to a low of one hour for unskilled workers.

The ETS study found that "Persons with high socioeconomic status tend to read more of all kinds of printed matter than those with low status." Similarly, the median reading time for IRA study participants in managerial and professional occupations was almost four times that for unskilled or unemployed workers.

While not indicating the amount of time spent reading daily, the NAEP study found that the overwhelming majority of respondents (85 percent) reported reading a newspaper and/or a magazine on a regular basis, reading and/or using a book within the previous six months, and using brief documents often.

What and When Do Adults Read?

The most commonly reported type of reading in all three studies was newspaper reading, with the vast majority of participants reporting reading newspapers on a regular basis. Street and traffic signs, billboards, and directions also accounted for a substantial amount of reading activity.

All three studies indicated that people in all demographic groups, whether broken down by occupation, race, educational level, or sex, read for information, political awareness, social development, and entertainment to varying degrees. The ETS study, which went into considerable detail as to the types and content of materials read by the adults in the study, did find considerable variation in the content and quality of materials read by persons of different socioeconomic status and educational level.

Following are some of the overall findings of the three studies; the three viewpoints give different but complementary information.

Education Testing Service (ETS), 1971

Table 6 shows the types of materials read and/or the activities during which reading took place, in descending order of frequency, as reported by the participants in the ETS study. The study found that 38 percent of the adults surveyed worked, and that a third of those read at work. Table 7 shows the items read while working, in order of frequency reported.

Of the respondents, 82 percent reported taking part in recreational and free-time activities during the week. Over half of them read during those activities; however, "by far, the most frequent kind of reading is the skimming of words and sentences on the TV screen by 38 percent of all adults." (Sharon 1973–1974, 166). The ETS study also found that the Bible was the single most

TABLE 6

What and When Do Adults Read?

ACTIVITY/ TYPE OF MATERIAL	PERCENT OF RESPONDENTS REPORTING	MEDIAN MINUTES/DAY
Newspaper	73	35
Traveling/street and traffic signs	70	3
Recreation	54	7
Mail	53	5
Magazines	39	33
Working around house	46	7
Mealtime	42	3
Books	33	47
At work	33	61
Shopping	33	7
Church/club activities	10	16
School	5	68
Theater/games/events	4	7

Source: Sharon (1973–1974), 161.

TABLE 7

Items Read While Working in Order of Frequency Reported

ITEM	MINUTES/DAY
Signs or notices	5
Letters, memos, or notes	16
Manuals and written instructions	17
Forms	21
Order forms, invoices, account statements	20
Schedules or lists	7
Telephone or address books	13
Reports, pamphlets, or articles in publications	19
Labels or writing on packages	6
Catalogs, brochures, or printed advertising	9
Specific work-related materials	30
Legal documents	30

Source: Sharon (1973–1974), 163.

frequently read book, being read by 5 percent of the respondents for an average of 29 minutes a day. Five percent of readers read general fiction, for an average of 46 minutes a day.

International Reading Association (IRA), 1982

The IRA study broke down reading by content type as well as by type of material. Tables 8 and 9 show the median reading time per day for each occupational group and for the total sample, first by content type, and then by type of material.

In Table 8, "Brief documents" includes bills/invoices, personal letters, newsletters/bulletins, labels or addresses on parcels, notices or signs on billboards, business correspondence, memos/notes, schedules/maps, forms filled out or read, files or records, legal documents, information for purchase (size, weight, contents), diagrams/charts, directions, and other. "Reference" includes manuals, directories, and items such as newspaper classified advertisements.

The IRA study also found that women, on the whole, read more than men (median time of 114 minutes/day for men vs. 186 minutes for women). Educational level was found to account for a considerable difference in reading time, as well: individuals with some post-secondary education read 217 minutes per day compared to a median time of less than 98 minutes per day for those with high school or less (Guthrie and Seifert 1983, 504).

National Assessment of Educational Progress (NAEP), 1985

The NAEP study asked participants about content areas read within newspapers and within magazines, books, and brief documents. The newspaper category included 13 content areas, including national/international and local news, comics, advertisements, sports, women's pages, financial news, book and movie reviews, and horoscopes. For magazines, respondents listed up to five different magazines they read on a regular basis and up to five that they read for their own enjoyment. Book content areas included fiction, history, science, recreation, entertainment, religion, references, and manuals. The brief documents category included 18 types of materials such as labels and tags, diagrams, tables, memos and notices, reports, and computer programs.

Reading activity was broken down by race, educational level, and parental educational level. The study found no differences

TABLE 8

What People Read, and How Much, by Occupation

CONTENT	OCCUPATIONAL GROUPS									
	1 PROFESSIONAL/ MANAGERIAL		2 SMALL BUSINESS/ CLERICAL		3 SKILLED CRAFTS WORKERS		4 UNSKILLED WORKERS		TOTAL	
	MEDIAN TIME[1]	PERCENT OF GROUP	MEDIAN TIME[1]	PERCENT OF GROUP	MEDIAN TIME[1]	PERCENT OF GROUP	MEDIAN TIME[1]	PERCENT OF GROUP	MEDIAN TIME[1]	PERCENT OF GROUP
News and business	32.5	100	11.5	100	20.2	100	8.5	90	17.8	98
Social issues	18.5	100	21.5	97	13.5	87	7.5	95	17.0	94
Sports/ recreation	3.5	83	3.5	75	6.5	80	3.0	75	4.1	78
Fiction	15.0	94	8.5	92	6.5	87	6.5	85	7.4	89
Reference	11.0	100	13.5	94	9.5	100	12.5	100	11.3	98
Brief documents	103.5	100	50.5	100	17.5	100	14.5	100	37.5	100
Total	224.5	100	173.5	100	108.5	100	60.0	100	157.5	100

Source: Guthrie and Seifert (1983), 503. Reprinted by permission of John T. Guthrie and the International Reading Association.

[1]Median minutes per day spent reading a particular type of content.

TABLE 9

Readership of Media by Demographic Groups

	MEDIAN MINUTES READ PER DAY		
OCCUPATION GROUP	NEWSPAPERS	BOOKS	MAGAZINES
1. Professional/managerial	40	36	19
2. Small business/clerical	39	33	8
3. Skilled worker	37	24	4
4. Unskilled/unemployed	37	3	3
Total	39	24	8

Source: Guthrie and Seifert (1983), 505. Reprinted by permission of John T. Guthrie and the International Reading Association.

among white, black, and Hispanic young adults with respect to the average number of content areas in newspapers and the average number of different books, magazines, or brief documents read. Nor were there significant differences based on respondents' educational levels or the educational levels of their parents. It should be noted, however, that the NAEP study did not address the amount of time spent reading or the quality of the materials being read.

The results of the content portion of the study are summarized in Table 10.

What Do Illiterates Want To Read?

As a footnote, it is interesting to note that the ETS study included people who could not read—5 percent of the total, including persons who were visually handicapped, foreign-language readers, and English-speaking persons who could not read at all (levels of literacy were not addressed). When asked what they would want to read if they could, most of the nonreaders named a specific type of material. The most frequently named type was religious, including items such as the Bible, Sunday school lessons, and prayers. Other items mentioned frequently included newspapers, magazines, books, and mail. Of the illiterates in the survey, 80 percent indicated that someone, usually a family member, read to them; the items most frequently mentioned were newspapers and mail (Sharon 1973–1974, 167–168).

TABLE 10

Average Number of Content Areas within Newspapers, and Different Magazines, Books, and Brief Documents Read by Race/Ethnicity, Educational Attainment, and Parental Education[1]

	NEWSPAPERS[2]	MAGAZINES[2]	BOOKS[2]	BRIEF DOCUMENTS[2]
Race/Ethnicity				
White	5.8 (3.0)	2.5 (1.6)	2.9 (2.0)	15.6 (7.7)
Black	5.6 (3.2)	2.6 (1.6)	2.3 (1.9)	12.1 (7.6)
Hispanic	5.7 (3.2)	2.4 (1.7)	2.3 (1.9)	13.8 (7.9)
Educational Attainment				
Less than high school	2.8 (3.2)	1.6 (1.3)	1.4 (1.7)	7.9 (5.9)
Some high school	4.7 (3.0)	2.0 (1.6)	1.4 (1.4)	8.8 (5.7)
High school graduate and/or some postsecondary	5.5 (3.0)	2.4 (1.6)	2.3 (1.8)	13.8 (7.1)
Postsecondary degree	6.6 (2.9)	2.9 (1.6)	4.0 (1.8)	19.0 (7.2)
Parental Education				
Less than high school	4.6 (3.4)	2.0 (1.6)	1.8 (1.6)	11.0 (7.0)
Some high school	4.8 (3.0)	2.1 (1.5)	1.9 (1.8)	11.0 (6.3)
High school graduate and/or some postsecondary	5.8 (3.1)	2.5 (1.6)	2.7 (1.9)	14.9 (7.4)
Postsecondary degree	6.3 (2.8)	2.9 (1.6)	3.6 (2.0)	18.0 (7.6)
Total	5.6 (3.1)	2.5 (1.6)	2.6 (2.0)	14.2 (7.8)

Source: Kirsch and Jungeblut (1986), 53. Reprinted by permission of Educational Testing Service.

[1]Figures in parentheses are standard deviations.

[2]Range: Newspapers — 0 to 13
Magazines — 0 to 5+
Books — 0 to 7
Brief Documents — 0 to 36

A Readability Comparison

It has become commonplace to rate both reading materials and reading ability in terms of grade level. In order to measure readability, a number of formulas, or indexes, have been developed. Generally, these formulas are based on a combination of factors that include the number of sentences, the number of words, and the number of "difficult" words in a sample passage. "Difficult" is variously defined, but is usually related to number of syllables. A detailed discussion of readability is outside the scope of this book. It is, however, interesting to compare the range of scores obtained for a single passage using the various popular formulas.

Table 11 compares the readability scores of 100-word sample passages taken from a variety of commonplace adult reading material. The sample passages used were from the following sources:

- [ ] The first three articles in the Bill of Rights
- [ ] Two samples from an issue of *Time* magazine: one from an international news story, the other from the "People" section
- [ ] Instructions for determining standard deductions on an Internal Revenue Service form
- [ ] A section on "Rules of the Road" from the *Colorado Drivers Manual*
- [ ] A passage from a best-selling novel (Judith Krantz's *Princess Daisy*)

The five indexes used were the Montana All-purpose Readability (MAR), the Fry, the Flesch, the Gunning Fog, and the Smog. The numbers indicate the presumed difficulty of the text in terms of grade level, i.e., years of education.

TABLE 11

Readability Scores of 100-Word Sample Passages

PASSAGE	MAR	FRY	FLESCH	FOG	SMOG
Bill of Rights	13.4	12.6	7.6	7.5	16.4
Time (international)	12.2	College	7.2	7.0	13.1
Time ("People")	9.6	11.5	8.2	7.5	12.5
IRS	College	College	9.1	12.2	14.3
Driver's manual	6.7	8.4	7.1	7.5	10.3
Princess Daisy	13.8	12.4	8.0	7.4	13.5

The wide score variations are in themselves an indication of the limited value of readability indexes. These formulas also fail to take into account important factors such as the reader's prior knowledge of, interest in, and motivation for reading about a particular subject matter; nor can they evaluate quality of writing. In fact, an assortment of garbled, choppy sentences with short words will measure as "more readable" (i.e., easier to read) than a well-written passage with compound sentences and polysyllabic words when, in fact, the opposite is true. Readability formulas, therefore, must be used in combination with good editorial judgment and an awareness of a potential reader's relationship to the material being evaluated.

A different type of readability index is the Degrees of Reading Power (DRP) scale. DRP measures readability in terms of a continuous scale. The difficulty of materials is calculated using a relatively complex formula that assigns points, or units, on a scale of 0 to 100 (the actual range of difficulty is from about 30 to about 80 units). The DRP scale avoids some of the problems associated with attempts to relate prose readability to grade level, a concept that becomes nearly meaningless when applied to adults. Nevertheless, the above cautions still apply.

Adult Education Legislation

The following is reprinted from *A History of the Adult Education Act,* published by the National Advisory Council for Education (Washington, DC, 1980), by permission of the National Advisory Council on Adult Education.

Adult Education Legislation: 1964-1978

Economic Opportunity Act of 1964

Legislative History

Title II, Part B,
Adult Basic
Education Programs
(P.L. 88–452)

S. 2642 introduced by Senator Patrick McNamara (Michigan) and 35 others and referred to the Committee on Labor and Public Welfare, March 16, 1964

- Reported with amendments, Senate Report No. 1218, July 8, 1964
- Supplemental Senate Report No. 1218, July 22, 1964
- Debated in Senate, July 21–23, 1964
- Amended and passed Senate, July 23, 1964
- Amended and passed House (in lieu of H.R. 11377), House Report No. 1458, August 8, 1964

- Senate concurs in House amendment, August 11, 1964
Signed by President Johnson, P.L. 88–452, August 20, 1964.

Purpose

It is the purpose of this legislation to initiate programs of instruction for persons 18 years old and older whose inability to read or write the English language constitutes a substantial impairment of their ability to obtain or retain employment.

Definitions

State educational agency. The state board of education or other agency primarily responsible for the state supervision of public elementary or secondary schools, or for adult education in public schools.

Local education agency: A public board of education or other public authority which has administrative control or direction of public elementary, secondary or adult schools of a political subdivision of a state.

Grants to States

The Director of the Office of Economic Opportunity was authorized to make grants to states to assist in:
—The establishment of pilot projects by local education agencies to demonstrate, test or develop special materials or methods of instruction; to stimulate the development of local educational agency programs for instruction; to acquire information concerning the materials or methods needed for an effective program for raising adult basic educational skills;
—meeting the cost of local educational agency programs for instruction of adults;
—development or improvement of technical or supervisory services by the state educational agency.

State Plans

In order to receive funds, each state was required to submit a plan which was to provide for:
—the administration of the program by the state educational agency;
—submission of reports to the Director of the Office of Economic Opportunity regarding the adult program;
—cooperative arrangements between the state educational agency and the state health authority to supply health information and services for participants in the program.

State Allotments

From the funds appropriated for this program, up to two per cent could be made available to Puerto Rico, Guam,

American Samoa, and the Virgin Islands. The remainder of the appropriated money would then be distributed to the states on the basis of the relative number of persons 18 years old and older in each state who had completed no more than five grades of school or its equivalent. No state could receive less than $50,000 and each state's allotment could be proportionately reduced to reach this $50,000 base.

The federal share for the adult education program was set at 90 percent for fiscal year 1966 and 50 per cent for fiscal year 1967.

Adult Education Act of 1966

Legislative History

Title IV
of the
1968 Amendments
to the
Elementary and Secondary
Education Act
and Related Amendments
(P.L. 90-247)

H.R. 13161 introduced by Congressman Carl D. Perkins (Kentucky) and referred to the Committee on Education and Labor, March 1, 1966

- Reported with amendments, House Report No. 1814, August 5, 1966
- Supplemental Report, House Report No. 1814, Part 2, August 27, 1966
- Made Special Order, House Resolution 1025, October 4, 1966
- Debated in the House, October 5–6, 1966
- Amended and passed the House, October 6, 1966
- Amended and passed the Senate (in lieu of S. 3046) Senate Report No. 89–1674, October 7, 1966
- House disagrees to Senate amendments and asks for a conference, October 10, 1966
- Senate insists on its amendments and agrees to a conference, October 17, 1966
- Conference report, House Report No. 2309, submitted in House and agreed to October 20, 1966
- Conference report submitted in Senate and agreed to October 22, 1966

Signed by President Johnson, P.L. 89–750, November 3, 1966

Purpose

It is the purpose of this legislation to encourage and expand basic educational programs for adults to enable them to overcome English language limitations, to improve their basic education in preparation for occupational training and more profitable employment, and to become more productive and responsible citizens.

Definitions

Adult: Any individual who has attained the age of eighteen.

Adult education: Services or instruction below the college level for adults who do not have a certificate of graduation from secondary school and are not currently enrolled in schools.

Adult basic education: Education for adults whose inability to speak, read, or write the English language constitutes a substantial impairment of their ability to get or retain employment, with a view to making them less likely to become dependent on others, to improving their ability to benefit from occupational training and otherwise increasing their opportunities for more profitable and productive employment, and to making them better able to meet their adult responsibilities.

Commissioner: The Commissioner of Education

Local education agency: A public board of education or other public authority which has administrative control or direction of public elementary, secondary or adult schools of a political subdivision of a state.

State: Includes the District of Columbia, the Commonwealth of Puerto Rico, Guam, American Samoa, the Trust Territory of the Pacific Islands, and the Virgin Islands.

State education agency: The state board of education or other agency primarily responsible for the state supervision of public elementary and secondary schools, or of adult education in public schools.

Grants to States

Not less than 10 per cent nor more than 20 per cent of the sums appropriated were reserved for special demonstration projects and teacher training (described below).

From the remainder of the appropriated funds, no more than two per cent could be distributed among Puerto Rico, Guam, American Samoa, the Trust Territory of the Pacific Islands, and the Virgin Islands.

Each state then received an amount distributed in relation to the proportion of adults in the state who had completed five grades of school or less.

In order to receive funds, each state was required to submit a plan setting forth a program which provides for:
—progress with respect to all segments of the adult population and all areas of the state;
—the administration of the plan by the state educational agency.
—cooperative arrangements between the state educational agency and the state health authority to make available health information and services for adults;
—grants to public and private nonprofit agencies for special projects, teacher training and research; and
—cooperation with community action programs, work experience programs, VISTA, work study and other programs relating to the antipoverty effort.

Payments

The federal share for each state could be used to pay up to 90 per cent of the cost of establishing or expanding adult basic education programs. Non-federal expenditures for each year could be no less than the amount expended during the preceding year.

Special Experimental Demonstration Projects and Teacher Training

Not less than 10 per cent nor more than 20 per cent of the funds appropriated were reserved to the Commissioner to make special project grants or to provide teacher training grants to local educational agencies and other public or private nonprofit agencies. Special experimental demonstration projects and teacher training grants require a non-federal contribution of at least 10 percent of the costs of such projects.

Special projects were defined as those involving the use of innovative methods, systems, materials, or programs of national significance or special value. Special project funds could also be used to carry out programs in cooperation with other federal, federally-assisted, state or local programs of unusual promise in promoting a comprehensive or coordinated approach to the problems of persons with basic educational deficiencies.

Grants for training persons engaged, or preparing to engage, as personnel in adult education programs could be provided to colleges or universities, state or local educational agencies, or other appropriate public or private nonprofit agencies or organizations.

Stipends and allowances were authorized for persons undergoing training.

Advisory Committee on Adult Basic Education

The Commissioner of Education was designated the chairman of a National Advisory Committee on Adult Basic Education. Seven additional members were to be appointed by the President.

The Advisory Committee was given the following responsibilities:

—to advise the Commissioner in the preparation of general regulations and policy matters relating to the administration of the Act, to the elimination of duplication and to the coordination of programs funded under this title with other adult education activities and services;

—to review the administration and effectiveness of the adult basic education program and other federally supported adult education programs; and

—to make annual reports to the President.

Summary of Major Revisions

Adult Education Act, 1966—1978

The major revisions in the Adult Education Act from 1966 to 1978 are reported in this section under the headings used in the legislation. The year and public law number have been included for each of the noted changes.

Statement of Purpose

P.L. 89–750 (1966):   to encourage and expand basic educational programs for adults to enable them to overcome English language limitations, to improve their basic education in preparation for occupational training and more profitable employment, and to become more productive and responsible citizens.

P.L. 91–230 (1970):   to expand educational opportunity and encourage the establishment of programs of adult public education that will enable all adults to continue their education to at least the level of completion of secondary school and make available the means to secure training that will enable them to become more employable, productive and responsible citizens.

P.L. 95–561 (1978):   to expand educational opportunities for adults and to encourage the establishment of programs of adult education that will:
—enable all adults to acquire basic skills necessary to function in society,
—enable adults who so desire to continue their education to at least the level of completion of secondary school, and
—make available to adults the means to secure training that will enable them to become more employable, productive, and responsible citizens.

Definitions

P.L. 89–750 (1966):   *Adult:* any individual who has attained the age of eighteen.

P.L. 91–230 (1970):   *Adult:* any individual who has attained the age of sixteen

added definitions of *academic education* and *institution of higher education*

P.L. 93–380 (1974):   added definition of *community school program*

P.L. 95–561 (1978):   *Adult:* (to be served by adult education) adds who "lack sufficient mastery of basic educational skills to enable them to function effectively in society."

Grants to States

P.L. 89–750 (1966):   established a distribution formula based on the proportion of adults in the state who had completed five grades of school or less.

P.L. 90–247 (1968):   provided a base allotment of $100,000 for each state; federal share of the cost of programs in the Trust Territory of the Pacific Islands was set at 100 per cent

P.L. 91–230 (1970): provided a base allotment of $150,000 for each state; established a distribution formula based on the proportion of adults not enrolled in school and who do not have a certificate of graduation from secondary school; authorized an additional appropriation, not to exceed five per cent of the sums appropriated for programs to pay the cost of administration and development of the state plan

P.L. 93–380 (1974): reduced the allotment for Guam, American Samoa, the Trust Territory of the Pacific Islands, and the Virgin Islands from two per cent to no more than one per cent of appropriated funds. The Commonwealth of Puerto Rico was defined as a state for the purposes of this section

Eligible Grant Recipients

P.L. 90–247 (1968): private nonprofit agencies were included as eligible grant recipients

Special Experimental Demonstration Projects and Teacher Training

P.L. 89–750 (1966): not less than 10 per cent nor more than 20 per cent of funds appropriated be reserved to the Commissioner to make special project grants or to provide teacher training grants

P.L. 93–380 (1974): 15 per cent of the state grant was to be used for special projects and for teacher training

P.L. 95–561 (1978): not less than 10 per cent of the state grant must be used for demonstration and teacher training. Special demonstration projects are specified as those which:
—involve the use of innovative methods, including methods for educating persons of limited English-speaking ability, systems, materials, or programs which may have national significance or be of special value in promoting effective programs under this title, or
—involve programs of adult education, including education for persons of limited English-speaking ability, which are part of community school programs, carried out in cooperation with other Federal, federally assisted, State, or local programs which have unusual promise in promoting a comprehensive or coordinated approach to the problems of persons with educational deficiencies.

State Plan Requirements

P.L. 91–230 (1970): provided that special emphasis be given to adult basic education programs

P.L. 93–380 (1974):   four requirements were added:
—programs for institutionalized adults
—provisions for cooperation with manpower development and training programs, occupational education programs and reading improvement programs
—not more than 20 per cent of state grant funds can be used for adult secondary programs
—special assistance for persons of limited English-speaking ability by providing bilingual programs

P.L. 95–561 (1978):   the law went into far greater detail in setting state plan requirements than earlier laws. These included:

—describe the means by which the delivery of adult education services will be significantly expanded through the use of agencies, institutions, and organizations other than the public school systems, such as business, labor unions, libraries, institutions of higher education, public health authorities, antipoverty programs, and community organizations;

—describe the means by which representatives of business and industry, labor unions, public and private educational agencies and institutions, churches, fraternal and voluntary organizations, community organizations, State and local manpower and training agencies, and representatives of special adult populations, including residents of rural areas, residents of urban areas with high rates of unemployment, adults with limited English language skills, and institutionalized adults, and other entities in the State concerned with adult education have been involved in the development of the plan and will continue to be involved in carrying out the plan, especially with regard to the expansion of the delivery of adult education services through those agencies, institutions, and organizations;

—describe the efforts to be undertaken by the State to assist adult participation in adult education programs through flexible course schedules, convenient locations, adequate transportation, and meeting child care needs;

—provide that special emphasis be given to adult basic education programs except where such needs are shown to have been met in the State;

—provide that special assistance be given to the needs of persons with limited English proficiency (as defined in section 703(a) of title VII of the Elementary and Secondary Education Act of 1965) by providing a bilingual adult education program of instruction in English and, to the extent necessary to allow such persons to progress effectively through the adult education program, in the native language of such persons, carried out in coordination with programs of bilingual education assisted under title VII and bilingual vocational education programs under the Vocational Education Act of 1963;

—demonstrate that the special educational needs of adult immigrants in the State have been examined, and provide for the implementation of adult education and adult basic education programs for immigrants to meet existing needs.

National Advisory Council on Adult Education

P.L. 89–750 (1966): established an eight-member Advisory Committee on Adult Basic Education

P.L. 91–230 (1970): established a 15-member National Advisory Council on Adult Education

Improvement of Educational Opportunities for Special Populations

P.L. 92–318 (1972): added a section authorizing programs for adult Indians

P.L. 93–380 (1974): authorized special projects for the elderly

P.L. 95–561 (1978): authorized special projects for Indochinese refugees and adult immigrants

State Advisory Councils

P.L. 93–380 (1974): established state advisory councils

Research, Development, Dissemination, Evaluation and Information Clearinghouse

P.L. 95–561 (1978): subject to appropriations, the Secretary of Education is authorized to conduct directly or through grants a wide variety of programs, including:
—develop new and promising approaches and innovative methods which are designed to address those problems and which may have national significance;
—determine, using appropriate objective evaluation criteria, which projects have achieved their stated goals and are capable of achieving comparable levels of effectiveness at additional locations;
—disseminate throughout the nation information about those approaches or methods pertaining to adult basic education which are most effective, by establishing and operating a clearinghouse on adult education, and evaluate the effectiveness of the programs conducted under this Act.

Selected Statistics of Adult Education State Grant Programs Aggregate United States, Fiscal Years 1965-1966, 1970, 1974-1980[1]

	FY 1965	FY 1966	FY 1970	FY 1974	FY 1975	FY 1976	FY 1977	FY 1978*	FY 1979*	FY 1980
	(Amounts in Thousands of Dollars)									
Federal Funds	$3,147	$32,562	$37,992	$59,526	$ 87,770	$ 67,500	$ 71,500	$ 80,500	$ 90,750	$100,000
State and Local	4,797	9,919	12,461	27,296	43,230	41,125	41,992	51,477	63,064	Not Available
TOTAL	$7,944	$42,481	$50,453	$86,822	$131,000	$108,625	$113,492	$131,977	$153,814	—
Number										
Enrollment	37,991	377,660	535,613	956,401	1,221,210	1,651,094	1,686,276	1,760,000	1,922,000	—
Percent of Annual Enrollment, By Sex										
Male	—	—	43	44	45	45	45	42	45	—
Female	—	—	57	56	55	55	55	58	55	—
TOTAL	—	—	100	100	100	100	100	100	100	—
Percent of Annual Enrollment, By Age Group										
16-24	—	15[2]	26[2]	37	40	42	41	41	41	—
25-34	—	26	27	27	28	27	27	27	27	—
35-44	—	27	24	18	16	16	16	16	16	—
45-54	—	20	13	10	9	8	9	9	9	—
55-64	—	10	7	5	4	4	4	4	4	—
65 & over	—	2	3	3	3	3	3	3	3	—
TOTAL	—	100	100	100	100	100	100	100	100	—

[1] Information on years not listed is available—U.S. Department of Education

[2] Includes only 18-24 year old enrollees

* Estimated

National Adult Literacy Congress

The following is a set of proclamations developed by delegates to the first National Adult Literacy Congress, held in September 1987 in Philadelphia.

September 10–11; Philadelphia, Pennsylvania; 1987; National Student Proclamations

The following proclamations, voiced by student representatives of adult literacy programs from the fifty states and the District of Columbia, address six important areas concerning the problem of illiteracy in the United States. Each statement was proclaimed to the nation in Congress Hall and unanimously approved by the delegates on 11 September 1987.

National Sponsors

- ☐ Lutheran Church Women
- ☐ Mayor's Commission on Literacy of Philadelphia
- ☐ Center for Literacy
- ☐ YMCA of Philadelphia
- ☐ Laubach Literacy Action

Who We Are: Educating the Public About Illiteracy

The term "illiterate" is here to stay, but it needs to be associated with positive ideas such as growth, dignity, pride, excitement in learning, and ongoing learning. Illiteracy should *not* be used to suggest dumb, stupid, diseased, or handicapped.

Short-term Education of the Public

Information should be more widely available and presented openly. More students need to come forward. Students should make their own statements. Actors should not be used. Information should be more specific; outreach groups could help with this. We need to be persistent in giving information to the public and show successful illiterate people.

Long-range Education of the Public

Information should show the educational benefits of literacy and the benefits to the next generation. Society needs to remove the time limit on learning and make a commitment to lifelong learning. Literacy should be seen as a right, not a privilege. People, especially the young, need to know that because of changes in society people need more education today.

Literacy and the Workplace

Companies

Companies need to be informed about the problems of illiteracy. When students go to companies and commit themselves to work on their GEDs, their rights must be protected. It should be illegal for an employer to fire someone who does not read. When students make a commitment to overcoming their reading problems, they should ask their employers for their help and commitment. Companies should encourage employees to seek help.

Students

Students should tell employers that they have made a sacrifice to learn to read and write. Students should take job-related materials to their tutors and study them with their tutors so they can know what their job is. Students should recruit other students on the job and encourage them to get help like we did.

Legislation

There should be tax credits for companies who help students.

Judicial System

We want judges to be aware of the problems of illiteracy. We want them to ask people who come before them: "Do you read and write?" We want the judges to tell people that help is available.

Legislation, Funding, and Resources for Literacy

People who cannot read have the right to an education. We are ambitious, creative, and talented individuals. However, we need the skills of reading and writing to be more productive. This learning is a shared responsibility between society and its citizens.

As a part of society's responsibility, it is critical that first, funding be increased to reach all illiterate people, and secondly, programs include support for tutors, teachers, materials, student participation, and outreach.

America needs all of us to solve today's problems and create the future.

Our Involvement in Issues of Literacy

We as students want a say in what is going on in the issues of literacy. We're the experts on issues of literacy because we've lived it. We can enrich an organization by being part of it. We can give programs information that they cannot get themselves. Other students can benefit by seeing new readers like themselves. We have lived it, and we can help students with some of the rough spots because we've been there. We, as students and new readers, want to be given the opportunity to work in our communities solving the illiteracy problem.

Literacy for Non–English Speaking Adults

We, the people of the United States, whose first language is from another country and who are learning English as a second language, wish to affirm and preserve our native languages, cultures, and histories. This is being done primarily in our homes: from grandparents to parents to children. To preserve our rich heritages, we use our native languages with our families, to teach cultural dances, to travel to our native lands, to cook our special foods, to tell stories, sing songs, and chant chants. We admire and hold our ancestors in great honor. We recommend the following actions to the nation:

- ☐ That teachers and tutors be given the best training possible: training based on *proven* and *effective* methods.
- ☐ That new readers help guide teachers and tutors in *what works* for students.
- ☐ That conversation be part of instruction.
- ☐ That wherever possible teachers and tutors from each ethnic group be recruited and trained to work with

their own people because they are especially sensitive to culture and language.

☐ That English-speaking teachers and tutors also be used with ethnic teachers and tutors.

☐ That each person needing to learn English be assessed at the level they need to begin.

☐ That a variety of learning methods be offered, including one-to-one tutoring and small group instruction.

☐ That this nation urge all citizens to learn more than one language, especially those languages of ethnic groups living in their own community.

What's Worked for Us

Every student is different. Everyone works at a different pace and has different needs, interests, and time available for lessons. However, there are some things that will help every student to succeed in learning.

Students can learn better if they have teachers and tutors who are dedicated to the student, have unselfish love and positive attitudes, can build self-confidence, and are well-trained to meet the needs of their particular students.

We believe that one-to-one works better because everyone can work at his or her own pace, it's more comfortable, you get more attention and much better results. We need the kinds of support we can get from tutors and teachers. They can help us with more than reading. They can help us read the Bible, do mathematics, write letters or checks; whatever we need.

We also need positive support from our families, friends, schools, and churches, indeed from everyone in public and private sectors, including the Congress.

We especially need support from other students. We need opportunities such as student support groups and student-teacher get togethers. We can "tell it like it is." We can teach some things that tutors and teachers cannot. We can cheer for each other and learn from each other.

Notes

1. Quoted in the *Harvard Educational Review,* 40 no. 2 (May 1970): 227.
2. Readers who wish to be more analytical are referred to the second chapter of Hunter and Harman's report, *Adult Illiteracy in the United States* (1979, 1985), for an in-depth discussion of literacy-related statistics.
3. Another important source of literacy information is the military, which has been involved in literacy and basic skills training throughout this century. Readers who wish to learn more about the information collected by the military are encouraged to obtain a copy of the report by Thomas Sticht et al., *Cast-off Youth: Policy and Training Methods from the Military Experience* (New York: Praeger, 1987).

4

Directory of Organizations, Associations, and Government Agencies

THIS IS A SELECTIVE LIST of nationally significant organizations, associations, and private and government agencies that are largely or wholly involved in literacy activities. Services and activities conducted by those listed include research, information services, public outreach, and volunteer training and assistance. Many other organizations that are not directly involved in literacy now have literacy task forces—these include the National Governors Association, the National Conference of Mayors, and the American Bar Association, among others. It would be impossible to list all of those groups here. Information about their activities is regularly reported in the newsletters listed in Chapter 5.

ACTION/VISTA Literacy Corps
806 Connecticut Avenue, NW
Washington, DC 20525
(202) 634-9445

The Volunteers in Service to America (VISTA) Literacy Corps was created by Congress in 1986 with a $2 million appropriation to supplement ongoing literacy activities within the VISTA program. The goals of the corps are to encourage partnerships, promote volunteerism, mobilize resources, increase the capacity of low-income communities to address their own literacy needs, heighten public awareness, and work toward development of a comprehensive strategy for combatting illiteracy. To these ends, VISTA Literacy Corps volunteers recruit and train tutors, perform outreach services, identify persons needing assistance, develop programs to teach literacy skills to refugees, organize or expand community-based literacy programs, and provide technical assistance in a variety of areas including fund raising.

PUBLICATIONS: *Literacy Forum Resource Package: A Resource Handbook* (1983), brochures, fact sheet.

Adult Learning Association
Star Route
Waterville, WA 98858
(509) 745-8287

The Adult Learning Association is a professional association of individuals and organizations involved in adult basic education, including instructors, tutors, counselors, libraries, and relatives and friends of persons in need of adult basic education. The association, which was founded in 1976, provides information on teaching methods, funding, and recruitment; promotes public awareness of adult basic education; and provides General Educational Development (GED) home study courses as well as workshops for parents, teachers, and tutors. It also sponsors the GED Institute, which specializes in information services related to GED tests. The association also issues annual awards to outstanding teachers, communicators, and students.

PUBLICATIONS: *Adult Basic Education Magazine* and *Adult Learner*, both quarterly; GED materials include a *GED Handbook,* predictive tests, *Warming up for the GED,* and *If I Don't Do This, I'll Never Do Anything.*

Adult Literacy and Technology Project
203 Rackley Building
University Park, PA 16802
(814) 863-3777

The Adult Literacy and Technology Project is a national project devoted to researching and promoting the integration of technology into adult literacy and adult basic education practice. The project is funded by the Gannett Foundation and coordinated by the Institute for the Study of Adult Literacy at the University of Pennsylvania. Areas of focus include development and evaluation of personal computer software, interactive video, interactive audio, reading machines, television, and radio. An important aspect of the project is the availability of regional technology consultants with expertise in both literacy and technology. The consultants are on call to literacy practitioners with questions or problems related to hardware, software, videos, etc. (call or write for the name of the consultant in your region). The project also awards subcontracts for research and program development in areas such as software evaluation and consultant training. The project held a national conference in June 1987 that featured approximately 60 presentations on topics including evolving technology, instruction, management, software, and staff development. About 300 literacy practitioners and researchers from all over the country attended.

PUBLICATIONS: newsletter (quarterly), LitLinc bulletin board; "Bibliotech," regularly updated bibliography available online through LitLine or by mail; *Conference Proceedings* (from June 1987 conference), includes presentation abstracts and directory of presenters.

Adult Literacy Initiative (ALI)
U.S. Department of Education
400 Maryland Avenue, SW
Washington, DC 20202
(202) 732-2959

The Adult Literacy Initiative (ALI) was established at the Division of Adult Education in 1983 to (1) generate national awareness; (2) promote public/private sector partnerships and encourage volunteerism; (3) provide technical and networking assistance; (4) coordinate federal literacy activities within the Department of Education and with other departments and agencies. Current activities include cooperating in the Coalition for Literacy/National Advertising Council literacy campaign; overseeing the Federal Employees Literacy Training (FELT), a federal employee volunteer recruitment program; College Work-Study Adult Literacy Project (to award supplemental grants to schools with established adult literacy programs), maintenance of LitLine computer communications network, research.

PUBLICATIONS: *ALI Update,* newsletter (four to six times/year), papers, reports.

American Association for Adult and Continuing Education (AAACE)
1201 16th Street, NW
Suite 230
Washington, DC 20036
(202) 822-7866

The American Association for Adult and Continuing Education (AAACE) is the nation's largest professional organization for adult educators and others associated with adult learning. It was formed in 1982 by the merger of the Adult Education Association of the U.S.A. (founded 1951) and the National Association for Public Continuing Adult Education (founded 1952). The goals of AAACE are (1) to provide leadership and unity in the profession of adult education; (2) to advocate adult and continuing education (including legislative influence); (3) to encourage research; (4) to share information. AAACE holds an annual conference and maintains a speakers' bureau. Its seven divisions include several subsidiary groups concerned with literacy and basic skills: the Commission on Adult Basic Education, the Adult Competency Education Unit, and the Council of State Directors of Adult Education. The National Adult Education Foundation (NAEF) funds "projects and activities of high priority for the Association and the field of adult and continuing education," including literacy projects.

PUBLICATIONS: *Lifelong Learning,* professional journal (monthly), *Adult Education Quarterly,* research and theory journal, *AAACE Newsletter* (monthly), annual membership directory, and a variety of resource publications including pamphlets, books, and monographs. Membership includes subscriptions to the newsletter and both journals.

American Association of Community and Junior Colleges (AACJC)
National Center for Higher Education
One Dupont Circle, NW
Suite 410
Washington, DC 20036
(202) 293-7050

Most of the approximately 1,200 member institutions of the American Association for Community and Junior Colleges (AACJC) offer basic skills programs for students and/or community residents. AACJC tracks the participation of its members in literacy activities, distributes information on national literacy efforts, and promotes legislation addressing adult literacy. The association recently conducted a national survey of literacy programs in community, technical, and junior colleges. In June 1987, AACJC, in conjunction with Project Literacy U.S. (PLUS) and IBM Educational Systems, sponsored a national teleconference on literacy in the work force.

PUBLICATIONS: *Community, Technical, and Junior College Journal* (bimonthly), newsletter (weekly), reports.

American Library Association (ALA)
Library Outreach Services
50 East Huron Street
Chicago, IL 60611
(312) 944-6780

The American Library Association (ALA) has, in effect, been promoting reading and literacy since its founding in 1876. With a membership of about 40,000 libraries and individual librarians, the ALA has links with local Adult Basic Education programs, volunteer programs, community colleges, and community-based organizations. The ALA encourages the development of literacy programs in libraries; provides training activities, information exchange, and directories; and was a founding member of the Coalition for Literacy. The Office of Library Outreach Services coordinates literacy activities. Other ALA units actively involved include the Public Library Association/Alternative Education Section; the Youth and Adult Services Division Committee on High Interest, Low-Literacy Level Materials Evaluation; and the American Library Trustee Association Task Force on Literacy Programs. Through national and local campaigns, the ALA works to prevent illiteracy by encouraging parents to read to their children and promotes reading through public service advertising.

PUBLICATIONS: handbooks, including *Literacy and the Nation's Libraries*; monographs and reports; brochures; fact sheet; promotional materials, including reading kits, posters, bookmarks, stickers, clip art, and print, radio, and television public service advertisements. Catalog available.

Assault on Illiteracy Program (AOIP)
410 Central Park West, PH-C
New York, NY 10025
(212) 967-4008

The national Assault on Illiteracy (AOIP) is a volunteer recruitment program aimed at alleviating illiteracy among black youth who have left school. AOIP maintains a network of 120 newspapers and 85 national organizations working to encourage blacks to get help with basic skills. AOIP's primary focus is on developing community leadership and instructional materials for distribution through black community newspapers and other publications.

Association for Community Based Education (ACBE)
1806 Vernon Street, NW
Washington, DC 20009
(202) 462-6333

The Association for Community Based Education (ACBE), which was founded in 1976, is a national association of independent community-based educational institutions. Programs offered by ACBE's approximately 60 member institutions include four-year accredited degree programs, job counseling, career preparation, and basic skills instruction. Through advocacy efforts and technical assistance to members, ACBE promotes alternative education programs that advance individual development and that involve a community development process. The association also communicates informally with thousands of community-based organizations serving an estimated 600,000 to 700,000 adults. ACBE's adult literacy efforts are primarily aimed at enhancing and strengthening community-based literacy organizations and literacy providers through the provision of services including technical assistance, financial support (including minigrants, scholarships, and loan guarantees), and training; networking; and support, monitoring, documentation, and evaluation of model and exemplary programs. ACBE holds an annual conference.

PUBLICATIONS: *Adult Literacy: Study of Community Based Literacy Programs* (rev. 1986), in two volumes, *Study Findings and Recommendations* and *Program Profiles*; *Directory of Corporate Funding Sources*; membership directory; fund-raising directory; *Standards of Performance for CBEIs*; newsletter, *The CBE Report* (biweekly); bulletins; reports.

Association of State Literacy Directors
c/o Kevin Smith, President
LVA of New York State
777 Maryvale Drive
Room 215
Buffalo, NY 14225
(716) 631-5282

The Association of State Literacy Directors is a professional organization/network for directors of state organizations working with volunteer programs. It provides support and assistance to states wishing to start such organizations, as well as serving as a forum for the exchange of ideas and information. The organization, which was officially founded (bylaws passed) in 1986 and has been unofficially in existence since about 1983, meets twice a year in various locations and charges dues of $100 a year.

Bilingual Education: Family English Literacy Program
Office of Bilingual Education and Minority Languages Affairs
U.S. Department of Education

400 Maryland Avenue, SW
Room 421
Washington, DC 20202
(202) 447-9228

The Family English Literacy Program provides assistance to local educational agencies, post-secondary institutions, and private nonprofit organizations for delivering a program of instruction designed to help limited English proficient adults and out-of-school youth achieve competence in the English language.

Business Council for Effective Literacy, Inc. (BCEL)
1221 Avenue of the Americas
New York, NY 10020
(212) 512-2415

The Business Council for Effective Literacy (BCEL) was founded in 1983 by publisher Harold McGraw, Jr., as a publicly supported foundation with the purpose of fostering greater corporate awareness of adult functional illiteracy and increasing business involvement in the literacy field. It provides technical assistance and guidance, working in both the public and private sectors. The BCEL newsletter is one of the best sources of current information on literacy research and practices.

PUBLICATIONS: newsletter (irregular); *BCEL Bulletin* (how-to guides for business literacy programs); *State Directory of Key Literacy Contacts; Turning Illiteracy Around: An Agenda for National Action,* set of two monographs; *Pioneers and New Frontiers,* monograph; *Functional Illiteracy Hurts Business,* leaflet. Write or call to be placed on mailing list.

Clearinghouse on Adult Education
U.S. Department of Education
Room 522, Reporters Building
400 Maryland Avenue, SW
Washington, DC 20202–5515
(202) 732-2396

The Clearinghouse on Adult Education provides a wide variety of materials related to adult education, including statistics, reports, directories, bibliographies, fact sheets, and resource guides. Materials are free, but limited to five articles per request.

PUBLICATIONS: materials available through the clearinghouse include *What Works in Adult Literacy* and *Promising Practices in Workplace Literacy,* both of which were due to be released in late 1987.

Coalition for Literacy
Coalition for Literacy Coordinator
American Library Association
50 East Huron Street
Chicago, IL 60611
(312) 944-6780

The Coalition for Literacy has a large membership that includes corporations, associations, and councils concerned with various aspects of literacy and adult education. In partnership with the Advertising Council, the coalition is sponsoring a nationwide three-year (beginning in 1986) literacy awareness media campaign consisting of television, radio, magazine, press, billboard, and hand-out materials designed primarily to recruit volunteer leaders and tutors. Materials are being printed, aired, and disseminated on a no-charge, public service basis. The campaign directs viewers, listeners, and readers to call the Contact Literacy Center's toll-free hotline for referrals and information.

Congressional Clearinghouse on the Future
555 House Annex 2
Washington, DC 20515
(202) 226-3434

The Congressional Clearinghouse on the Future is a legislative service organization that explores policy implications of emerging demographic, technological, and economic trends and develops projects on specific issues during each session of Congress; literacy has been a recent focus. Services to members include: dialogue series involving members of Congress and well-known leaders and analysts; regional projects and conferences; scanning services that monitor and report trends; and tailored services involving staff briefings, news and photo releases, and networks of experts, pollsters, and press contacts.

PUBLICATIONS: *Emerging Issues* briefing papers, *New Ideas* memos, *What's Next* newsletter (quarterly).

Contact Literacy Center
P.O. Box 81826
Lincoln, NE 68501–1826
(402) 464-0602
(800) 228-8813

The Contact Literacy Center serves as the information clearinghouse for the Coalition for Literacy and Project Literacy U.S. (PLUS), providing, via its toll-free hotline, referrals and general literacy information, including statistics, how-to advice for current and potential program directors, volunteer opportunities, etc. Begun in 1978 as a project of the American Association of Advertising Agencies (AAAA), the center is still affiliated with AAAA through the Coalition for Literacy. Contact Literacy maintains a database of more than 6,500 literacy resources and 7,000 human service agencies nationwide.

PUBLICATIONS: directory, *Reducing Functional Illiteracy: A National Guide to Facilities and Services* (revised annually); newsletter, *the written word* (monthly); brochures, fact sheets, reports.

Correctional Education Association (CEA)
4321 Hartwick Road
Suite L-208
College Park, MD 20740
(301) 277-9088

Founded in 1946, the Correctional Education Association (CEA) is an international professional association for educators and administrators involved in providing education, including literacy instruction, to students in correctional settings. In addition to networking, technical assistance, and advocacy, the association provides consulting services in both the public and private sectors. CEA holds an annual conference; locations vary.

PUBLICATIONS: *Journal of Correctional Education, CEA Newsletter* (both quarterly); *Lobbying for Correctional Education: A Guide to Action,* monograph.

Division of Adult Education
U.S. Department of Education
400 Maryland Avenue, SW
Washington, DC 20202
(202) 732-2959

The Division of Adult Education has as its primary goal the establishment of programs that will (1) enable adults (i.e., those 16 or older) to acquire the basic literacy skills necessary to function in society; (2) enable adults to continue their education through at least the level of secondary school completion; (3) make available to adults the means to secure training and education that will enable them to become more employable, productive, and responsible citizens. The division provides assistance to state educational agencies, which in turn fund local delivery systems, including local educational agencies and public or private organizations and institutions.

Education Commission of the States (ECS)—Adult Literacy Project
1860 Lincoln Street
Suite 300
Denver, CO 80295
(303) 830-3627

The Education Commission of the States (ECS) is a compact of states and territories that assists state political and education leaders in developing education policy. ECS maintains an information clearinghouse, provides technical assistance, conducts research, and organizes state, regional, and national forums on various education issues, including literacy. The ECS Adult Literacy Project is a lobbying group aimed at focusing attention of governors and other state education policy makers on the literacy issue and the need for increased funding.

PUBLICATIONS: *Adult Literacy* (video for governors and state policy makers).

Educational Resources Information Center (ERIC) Clearinghouse on Adult, Career, and Vocational Education
Ohio State University
1960 Kenney Road
Columbus, OH 43210–1090
(800) 848-4815
(614) 486-3655 in Ohio

ERIC Clearinghouse on Reading and Communications Skills
1111 Kenyon Road
Urbana, IL 61801
(217) 328-3870

ERIC Clearinghouse on Library and Information Resources
Syracuse University
School of Education
Huntington Hall, Room 030
Syracuse, NY 13210
(315) 423-3640

The Educational Resources Information Center (ERIC) is a national education information system sponsored by the Office of Educational Research and Improvement, U.S. Department of Education. ERIC offers some of the best access to comprehensive information in all areas of education, including literacy and adult education. ERIC facilities include a network of 16 clearinghouses, which distribute information in specialized fields of education; a central editorial and computer facility, which maintains the ERIC database (see Chapter 6) and prepares the abstract journal *Resources in Education*; a document reproduction service; and a commercial publisher, the Oryx Press, whose publications include *Current Index to Journals in Education* and the *Thesaurus of ERIC Descriptors*. ERIC services include abstracts, article and report reproduction (hard copy or microfiche), general information, computer searches, and referrals to other resources. Many materials are available at little or no cost. Two of the ERIC clearinghouses specialize in information areas related to adult literacy. The ERIC Clearinghouse on Adult, Career, and Vocational Education provides comprehensive information services in the areas of adult and continuing education (including literacy and basic skills education), career education, and vocational and technical education. The ERIC Clearinghouse on Reading and Communications Skills provides information services related to education in reading, English, and communications skills. The ERIC Clearinghouse on Library and Information Resources provides detailed information about ERIC itself, including information on accessing the database, submitting documents, and obtaining materials.

PUBLICATIONS: *Resources in Education (RIE)* (abstracts from research reports, curriculum guides, program descriptions, etc.), and *Current Index to Journals in Education* (citations and annotations of articles from educational periodicals), both monthly; newsletters (offered by the individual clearinghouses); short bibliographies (Minibibs) on selected topics; digests, packaged searches on high-interest topics; reports and papers; columns and articles in professional journals.

Gannett Foundation
Lincoln Tower
Rochester, NY 14604
(716) 262-3315

Literacy programs are an ongoing focus of the Gannett Foundation, one of the 20 largest private foundations in the United States. Between 1980 and 1987, the foundation contributed more than $3.5 million to programs and projects aimed at increasing literacy and teaching English to immigrants. Grant recipients included special initiatives, pilot projects, and start-up programs around the country. In 1986, the foundation, in cooperation with *USA Today,* launched the Literacy Challenge, a two-year $2 million competitive state-level grants program aimed at increasing the effectiveness of adult literacy programs in the United States. In its first year, the program awarded grants ranging from $40,000 to $100,000 to projects in 12 states and Puerto Rico. Goals of the program were to (1) strengthen statewide literacy efforts through coordination of agencies; (2) teach more adults to read through increased volunteer involvement; (3) increase resources available to literacy agencies; (4) generate increased public awareness and encourage community efforts.

PUBLICATIONS: annual reports, grant application guidelines, *Media Resource Guide.*

Give the Gift of Literacy
American Booksellers Association, Inc.
122 East 42nd Street
New York, NY 10168
(612) 893-7203

Give the Gift of Literacy is a fund-raising organization cosponsored by the American Booksellers Association (ABA) and Telephone Pioneers of America to promote awareness and to raise money for adults' and children's literacy efforts such as the Coalition for Literacy and Reading Is Fundamental (RIF). The campaign raises funds primarily through coin boxes placed in bookstores around the country.

PUBLICATIONS: pamphlet.

Institute for the Study of Adult Literacy
Pennsylvania State University
College of Education
301 Rackley Building
University Park, PA 16802
(814) 863-3781

The Institute for the Study of Adult Literacy was established in 1985 for the purpose of filling the gaps in the existing research literature, forming a sound conceptual and research base for literacy efforts, and advocating adult literacy. A major emphasis is on the use of technology and media in adult literacy instruction and staff development. For example, the Adult Literacy and Technology Project, begun in 1985 and funded by the Gannett Foundation, is coordinating efforts to integrate technology into adult literacy/adult basic education programs. Other projects include a television in-service series for adult basic education teachers and literacy tutors, a video series for pre-GED–level adults, an inventory of media-based instructional materials, courseware development, and a manual for libraries planning literacy programs.

PUBLICATIONS: newsletter, monograph series, videos, manuals, reports.

International Reading Association (IRA)
800 Barksdale Road
P.O. Box 8139
Newark, DE 19714–8139
(302) 731-1600

The International Reading Association (IRA) was founded in 1956 with these aims: to improve reading instruction at all educational levels through research and teacher education, to promote reading as a lifetime habit, and to increase awareness of the impact of reading. Membership consists of persons involved in reading instruction at any school level. The association recently formed a special interest group for vocational education, with an emphasis on supporting reading and language development in the context of vocational education. Citations and awards issued by the IRA include the annual IRA Literacy Award for outstanding contributions to literacy. The association holds an annual conference in the spring.

PUBLICATIONS: *Reading Teacher* (nine times/year); *Journal of Reading* (eight times/year); *Lectura y Vida* (quarterly); *Reading Research* (quarterly); subscriptions to all of these included with membership or available separately. The IRA also publishes eight to ten books and monographs annually.

Laubach Literacy Action (LLA)—New Readers Press
1320 Jamesville Avenue
P.O. Box 131
Syracuse, NY 13210
(315) 422-9121

Laubach Literacy Action (LLA) is the U.S. volunteer membership arm of Laubach Literacy International (LLI), which was incorporated in 1955 as a continuation of the work of Dr. Frank Laubach; the Canadian arm is Laubach Literacy of Canada. LLA provides training and supervised certification in reading, teaching English for Speakers of Other Languages (ESOL), and writing for new readers. The Laubach Method and materials, based on a carefully sequenced, phonetic approach, are used by some 50,000 volunteers in over 600 projects in 46 states. LLA provides leadership and program management training for program administrators and organizers, along with information and referral services and technical and fund-raising assistance. LLA promotes adult literacy services through local and national media and through contacts with national and state agencies.

PUBLICATIONS: Laubach Literacy International (LLI) maintains its own publishing division, New Readers Press, which publishes a wide variety of training, promotional, program management, and reading materials, including books, manuals, workbooks, software, video and audio materials, and periodicals for practitioners, tutors, and students. Topics include health, children, government, economics, social studies, science, and money management, as well as basic skills and pleasure reading. Catalogs are available. LLA also publishes an annual directory of local literacy programs; to be included, programs must register and pay a fee.

Library Literacy Program
Library Development Staff
Office of Educational Research and Improvement
U.S. Department of Education
1200 19th Street, NW
Washington, DC 20208–1730
(202) 254-5890

The Library Literacy Program provides assistance to state and local public libraries for planning and coordinating library literacy programs, training librarians and volunteers, and acquiring materials. The program provided nearly $5 million worth of assistance in 1986.

Literacy Volunteers of America, Inc. (LVA)
404 Oak Street
Syracuse, NY 13203
(315) 445-8000

Founded in 1962 by Syracuse housewife Ruth Colvin, Literacy Volunteers of America (LVA) is a national, nonprofit organization that provides training, materials, technical assistance, and ongoing support to nonprofessional volunteer tutors providing basic skills and English for Speakers of Other Languages (ESOL) training in over 200 programs in 32 states. LVA works in conjunction with correctional facilities, Adult Basic Education (ABE) programs, schools, universities, libraries, industry, and other community service programs to recruit and train volunteers and provide literacy services. LVA's materials and methods are designed to meet varying needs and interests of individual students, using various combinations of language experience, sight words, phonics, and patterned word techniques.

PUBLICATIONS: newsletter, *The Reader* (quarterly); LVA also publishes a variety of training and program management materials, including books, bibliographies, handbooks, workbooks, and video and audio tapes. LVA's Adult Literacy Series, developed under a grant from the National Endowment for the Humanities and published by Cambridge

Book Company, includes adult-interest stories, poems, and essays for beginning readers, as well as a teacher's guide. Catalog available.

Lutheran Church Women (LCW)
See Women of the Evangelical Lutheran Church in America (WELCA)

National Advisory Council on Adult Education
200 L Street, NW
Suite 570
Washington, DC 20036
(202) 634-6300

The National Advisory Council on Adult Education is a presidentially appointed council set up to advise Congress and the administration concerning policies related to the Adult Education Program.

PUBLICATIONS: annual reports include *A History of the Adult Education Act* (1980); *Opening Doors for Success* (1983); *Illiteracy in America: Extent, Causes, and Suggested Solutions* (1986).

National Diffusion Network (NDN)
Division of Recognition
Office of Educational Research and Improvement
U.S. Department of Education
Room 714, Brown Building
1200 19th Street, NW
Washington, DC 20036
(202) 653-7000

The National Diffusion Network (NDN) is a federally funded system that makes exemplary educational projects available for adoption by adult education and other programs and institutions. NDN provides dissemination funds to projects in order to enable the projects to (1) make educators aware of services; and (2) provide in-service training, followup assistance, and materials to educational programs that want to adopt them. NDN also provides funds to state facilitators, whose role is to serve as matchmakers between NDN projects and adult education programs that could benefit by adopting the projects. A wide range of basic skills and literacy-related projects are available for adoption through NDN. Programs funded in 1986 included the nationally recognized Jefferson County (Kentucky) Adult Reading Program (JCARP), which uses community linkages and volunteers to deliver literacy and life coping skills instruction, and the Comprehensive Adult Student Assessment System (CASAS), which provides adult education agencies with assessment materials and procedures to develop a competency-based life skills program.

PUBLICATIONS: *Adopting NDN Projects* (guide includes project descriptions, list of state facilitators).

National Institute of Corrections Information Center—Clearinghouse for Offender Literacy Programs
1790 30th Street
Suite 130
Boulder, CO 80301
(303) 444-1101

The National Institute of Corrections Information Center serves as a clearinghouse for a variety of information and materials for educators of students in correctional settings. Materials are free upon request and include the procedures used to implement the state of Virginia's "no read no release" literacy incentive program and two U.S. Department of Education reports: *Literacy Training in Penal Institutions* and *Evaluation Research in Basic Skills with Incarcerated Adults*.

National Issues Forum (NIF)
NIF-Laubach Pilot Project
5335 Far Hills Avenue
Dayton, OH 45429
(513) 434-7300
(800) 221-3657
(800) 523-0078 in Ohio

The National Issues Forum (NIF) is a nationwide issues discussion program sponsored by the Domestic Policy Association, a nonpartisan citizen-based network of civic and educational institutions. Its purpose is to provide citizens with an opportunity to discuss complex national issues in order to identify areas of common ground. Three topics are chosen each year for the next year's forum discussions (sample: "Crime: What We Fear, What Can Be Done"). The NIF-Laubach Pilot Project is aimed at enabling low-literate individuals to participate in the forum through specially written materials and outreach programs. In addition to providing participants with a voice, the project offers students a reason to learn to read and write.

PUBLICATIONS: brochure, NIF issue books (written at 4.5 to 6.5 grade level).

Project Literacy U.S. (PLUS)
PLUS Project Director
4802 Fifth Avenue
Pittsburgh, PA 15213
(412) 622-1491

Project Literacy U.S. (PLUS) is a national media/outreach campaign cosponsored by the American Broadcasting Company, Inc. (ABC), the Public Broadcasting Service (PBS), their affiliates, and numerous community groups, including educational organizations, literacy organizations, businesses, media, and community services. Events produced and/or sponsored by PLUS include television documentaries, special features, and public service announcements; outreach programs; and other activities, including national teleconferences. The campaign began in 1986 with the goals of raising national awareness of the problem of adult functional illiteracy in America; developing and encouraging volunteer action to address illiteracy; and encouraging those who can help and those who need help to participate. The 1987–1988 themes for the campaign are civic literacy, literacy in the work force, and literacy and youth.

PUBLICATIONS: *Information and Resources for Task Forces, Literacy Video Resources Guide*, newsletter, brochures, posters.

Reading Is Fundamental, Inc. (RIF)
Smithsonian Institution
Room 500
600 Maryland Avenue, SW
Washington, DC 20560
(202) 287-3371

Founded in 1966 by Margaret McNamara, Reading Is Fundamental, Inc. (RIF) is the largest reading motivation program in the United States. An affiliate of the Smithsonian Institution, RIF is a national nonprofit organization dedicated to preventing illiteracy by motivating children to read. Through a nationwide volunteer network of more than 90,000 parents, educators, librarians, and business and civic leaders, RIF enables over two million children annually, in all 50 states, to choose and own books at no cost to themselves or their families. RIF also provides publications and services to help parents encourage reading at home and promotes reading through public service media campaigns.

PUBLICATIONS: newsletter (three times/year); *Book of Booklists*; *The RIF Book of Ideas* (activities for parents); posters; variety of brochures (sample titles: "Reading Aloud to Your Children," "TV and Reading,"

"Choosing Good Books"); film, *Reading Is Fundamental*; various technical assistance materials for volunteers.

Urban Literacy Development Fund
7505 Metro Boulevard
Minneapolis, MN 55435
(612) 893-7661

The Urban Literacy Development Fund was formed in 1987 as a partnership project by ACTION, the national volunteer agency; the Gannett Foundation; the Dayton Hudson Corporation; and B. Dalton Bookseller, with the Minneapolis Foundation as fiscal agent. The purpose of the fund is to provide grants, communication, training, and advocacy in support of literacy efforts in urban areas, with a focus on improving the use of existing public and private resources while generating new ones. First-year efforts included building a national network of urban-based literacy programs and supporters through written updates, electronic bulletin boards, and a directory of urban literacy contacts; and funding collective efforts aimed at increasing public, private, and volunteer resources in ten demonstration sites in urban areas.

Women of the Evangelical Lutheran Church in America (WELCA)
Director of Literacy
8765 West Higgins Road
Chicago, IL 60631

In 1987, the Lutheran Church Women (LCW) merged with the Women of the Evangelical Lutheran Church in America (WELCA). From 1969 to 1987, the Lutheran Church Women had an active Volunteer Reading Aides Program that conducted promotional activities and provided training, materials, and technical assistance to basic skills and English for Speakers of Other Languages (ESOL) volunteer tutors and organizations throughout North America. The Volunteer Reading Aides Program will continue under WELCA, which has identified literacy as an important focus of its "Mission in Action" programming.

PUBLICATIONS: *Churches and Literacy* (1988). LCW publications that will also be available through WELCA include *Handbook for Volunteer Reading Aides* (1984), plus films and videos.

World Education, Inc. (WEI)
210 Lincoln Street
Boston, MA 02111
(617) 482-9485

World Education, Inc. (WEI), a private, volunteer organization founded in 1951 and incorporated in 1957, provides training and technical assistance in nonformal education for adults, with special emphases on income generation, community development, small enterprise development, literacy, food production, and family life education. WEI conducts a variety of literacy projects throughout the world. One current focus is the development of a master's-level program in literacy at the University of Massachusetts, which will include a summer training program to make the curriculum available to those who do not have the time to pursue a degree.

PUBLICATIONS: *Adult Illiteracy in the United States,* produced from a study funded by the Ford Foundation; *Reports Magazine* (quarterly), which is devoting an issue per year (1987–1989) to the topic of literacy; *Focus on Basics,* a resource bulletin for teachers in programs providing basic skills training to adults.

5

Reference Materials

THE FOLLOWING IS A HIGHLY selective and rather eclectic bibliography of reference works, including bibliographies, handbooks, yearbooks, significant books and monographs, and periodicals. It includes scholarly works, government and privately produced reports, and more popularly oriented works ranging from the theoretical to the practical. The emphasis is on literacy/illiteracy as subject, rather than on instructional techniques and training per se. The works cited present widely varying viewpoints and analyses. Although the annotations cannot avoid being somewhat subjective, it is ultimately left to the reader to decide the validity of any given point of view. Prices and ISBNs are included where available.

Bibliographies

Buckingham, Melissa Forinash, comp. **The New Reader Development Bibliography: Books Recommended for Adult New Readers,** 3d ed.
Syracuse, NY: New Readers Press, 1982.
86p. $15.95. Distributed by R. R. Bowker Company.

The compiler of this annotated, graded bibliography of books for adult new readers and tutor resource materials writes a regular column for *Booklist,* in which she reviews materials for low-reading-level adults.

111

The bibliography includes titles graded at the eighth-grade level or below according to the Gunning Fog Index. Topics include basic and intermediate skills and pre-GED. An appendix on materials for deaf adults is also included.

Graff, Harvey J. **Literacy in History: An Interdisciplinary Research Bibliography (Garland Reference Library of the Humanities,** vol. 254).
New York: Garland, 1981.
422p. Index. $61. ISBN 0–8240–9460–3.

Harvey Graff is a scholar and researcher who has devoted a large part of his career to literacy studies. The entries in this extensive bibliography are grouped according to topic, including historical approaches, family studies, crime and criminality, and studies of women and minorities. *Literacy in History* is a comprehensive research tool for social, economic, and educational historians; social scientists; and educationist theory and policy makers concerned with literacy.

Heiser, Jane-Carol. **Literacy Resources: An Annotated Checklist for Tutors and Librarians.**
Baltimore: Enoch Pratt Free Library, 1983.
144p. Index. $5. ISBN 0–910556–19–9.

This annotated bibliography, compiled by a resource librarian, lists a variety of materials for adult new readers and tutors, including workbooks, ditto masters, teacher's guides, newspapers, and audiovisual materials, most geared to reading levels below seventh grade. Areas covered include basic English and study skills, life skills (e.g., jobs and child care), and leisure reading. Two sections of tutor resources include teaching guides, training materials, and manuals, plus a variety of reference sources.

Kasemek, Francis E., and Pat Rigg, comps. **Adult Illiteracy: An Annotated Bibliography.**
Newark, DE: International Reading Association, 1984.
36p. $3. ISBN 0–87207–340–8.

The compilers question the current emphasis on "survival" skills such as filling out forms and applications, believing that the reason adults read and write is to understand and control their world. Intended for literacy workers, teacher trainers, and program developers and directors, this bibliography includes easy-to-obtain journal articles, books, and Educational Resources Information Center (ERIC) reports. The compilers included items to exemplify the above philosophy (with the exception of some "influential works"), items directed at the intended audience, and items with immediate and long-term relevancy. Entries are divided into five sections: State of Adult Literacy, Ways of Looking at Literacy, Critiques of Some Current Philosophical Assumptions about Literacy, Research, and Training.

MacDonald, Barbara J., and V. K. Lawson, eds. **Core Library for Literacy and Conversational English Programs.**
Syracuse, NY: Literacy Volunteers of America, 1984.
34p. $5. LVA, 404 Oak Street, Syracuse, NY 13203.

This annotated bibliography is intended primarily for LVA tutors and program directors; librarians may find it useful for identifying materials. The entries were selected by a panel of tutors, librarians, trainers, and materials specialists. Titles are indexed by reading level. The book also includes a list of publishers' addresses and sections on materials selection for basic reading and conversational English.

Project: LEARN. **Books for Adult New Readers,** 3d ed.
Cleveland, OH: Project LEARN, 1986.
301p. Index. Spiralbound. $10 (includes postage and handling). Project LEARN, 2238 Euclid Avenue, Cleveland, OH 44115.

This is the third revised edition of this popular annotated bibliography of print materials for English-speaking adults. Most of the materials can be read or used by adult new readers with minimal assistance; 62 percent are at fifth-grade reading level or lower, and most of the remainder are at seventh-grade level. More than 95 percent of the titles are paperback. The more than 500 titles were selected for broad appeal to adult new readers; nonfiction entries include works on useful subjects such as consumer economics, occupational guidance, health, government, and skills development, while leisure reading selections include a wide variety of fiction, literature, and biographies. This edition includes a listing of core collection recommendations, an annotated list of series, a list of "already at the library" readings, and lists of suggested readings for librarians and tutors. Author and subject indexes and a list of publishers' addresses (with toll-free numbers, where available) are also included.

Handbooks

Bayley, Linda. **Opening Doors for Adult New Readers: How Libraries Can Select Materials and Establish Collections.**
Syracuse, NY: New Readers Press, 1980, rev. 1984.
17p. Free.

This free handbook for librarians provides information on determining the needs of adult new readers; identifying the types of materials to provide; locating, selecting, and purchasing materials; organizing the collection (which the author recommends keeping separate from the regular library collection); providing programs for new readers; and publicizing the materials and programs in the community.

Council of State Policy and Planning Agencies (CSPA). **Adult Literacy for Jobs and Productivity: A Policy Guide.**
Washington, DC: CSPA, 1987.
CSPA, 400 North Capitol Street, NW, Suite 291, Washington, DC 20001.

This well-researched and thoughtfully written guide is designed to assist state policy and planning officials in addressing the issues of adult literacy by exploring the relationship of literacy, jobs, and productivity. The primary focus is on improving labor force skills in order to develop and maintain healthy state economies, with an emphasis on policies and approaches at the gubernatorial level. The guide offers an excellent overview of the problems of defining and measuring literacy and of the complex issues involved in designing, planning, and implementing effective literacy programs that address real needs. It also details practical suggestions for approaches and actions to be taken at a state level.

Cross, K. Patricia. **Adults as Learners: Increasing Participation and Facilitating Learning.**
San Francisco: Jossey-Bass, 1981.
300p. Bibliography. Index. ISBN 0–87589–491–7.

The author characterizes this as a "how-to-think-about-it" rather than a how-to-do-it book. The book focuses on these key questions about adult learning: who participates and why or why not, and what and how do they learn and want to learn. The first six chapters examine demographic, social, and technological trends that are stimulating the demand for learning opportunities; issues involved in recruiting adult learners; the characteristics of adult learners; and motivations and deterrents to adult learning. The remaining chapters critically examine and synthesize existing research about what and how adults learn and suggest a conceptual framework for analyzing the ways in which learners interact with their environments. Two appendixes include a collection of definitions of and comments about lifelong learning and a list of characteristics of lifelong education. Although not specifically concerned with literacy education, this book provides a useful overview of the factors and issues involved in any kind of adult learning situation.

Harman, David. **What Works in Adult Literacy.**
Washington, DC: U.S. Department of Education, Adult Literacy
Initiative, 1987.
Clearinghouse on Adult Education, U.S. Department of Education,
Room 522, 400 Maryland Avenue, SW, Washington, DC, 20202–5515.

What Works in Adult Literacy is part of a series produced by the Department of Education detailing what works in education. Written by David Harman with the help of a 16-member advisory committee, the booklet discusses components of successful literacy programs and describes both practices that work and practices that don't in programs around the country. It also contains practical advice and suggestions for effective practices, along with summaries of existing research, new findings, and a detailed list of literacy program contacts.

Jones, Edward. **Reading Instruction for the Adult Illiterate.**
Chicago: American Library Association, 1981.
169p. Index. ISBN 0–8389–0317–7.

The first part of this book is a discussion of functional illiteracy as a social problem in the United States, including the ways different ideas of what constitutes illiteracy have affected its statistical representations, and the environmental and motivational factors involved in learning by adult illiterates. The second part offers practical, language-based strategies for teaching adults to read, based on what is known about the ways adult illiterates learn and on a research-supported view of the processes involved in learning to read.

Knowles, Malcolm S. **The Modern Practice of Adult Education:**
From Pedagogy to Andragogy.
Chicago: Follett, 1980.
400p. Index. ISBN 0–695–81472–9.

Malcolm Knowles is an acknowledged leader in the field of adult learning. This guidebook offers a thorough overview of both the theory and the practice of *andragogy,* a word Dr. Knowles coined to describe "the new technology of adult education." First published in 1970, *Modern Practice* was extensively revised and rewritten a decade later, and reflects recent changes in philosophy and approach to education. Most notably, these include a change in emphasis from "knowledge" to "competence," a shift from a focus on teaching to a focus on learning, and the emerging concept of learning as a lifelong activity, with a corresponding change in how educational services are delivered. Topics range from the psychological and philosophical (a discussion of adult education in relation to the need for individual self-development) to the practical (planning meeting spaces). The book's 11 appendixes include sample program designs, tools for operating programs, and evaluation materials.

Laubach, Frank, and Kay Koschnick. **Using Readability: Formulas for Easy Adult Materials.**
Syracuse, NY: New Readers Press, 1977.
40p. $2.75.

This forty-page guide by the founder of Laubach Literacy International explains how to apply the Gunning Fog Index and the Fry Readability Graph and discusses the factors that make books easy to read.

Lerche, Renee S. **Effective Adult Literacy Programs: A Practitioner's Guide.**
New York: Cambridge Book Company, 1985.
282p. Bibliography. Index. $24.95. ISBN 0–8428–2219–4.

This guidebook represents a synthesis of the findings of the National Adult Literacy Project's 1984 Promising Practices Search, a survey of 225 programs in 43 states, the District of Columbia, Puerto Rico, and the Virgin Islands, plus one Canadian program. The study included on-site visits to 38 of the responding programs. Programs studied were in six categories: (1) state and local public adult education programs; (2) community-based programs; (3) programs operating inside correctional institutions; (4) military-based programs; (5) programs in post-secondary educational institutions; (6) employment and training programs. The book includes sections on Components of Effective Programs (including Orientation, Counseling, Diagnostic Testing and Assessment, Instructional Methods and Materials, Follow-up of Learners, and Program Evaluation); Conclusions for Practitioners; and Networking.

Library of Michigan. **Libraries and Literacy: A Literacy Handbook.**
Lansing, MI: Library of Michigan, 1986.
27p. Free. Library of Michigan, 735 East Michigan Avenue, P.O. Box 30007, Lansing, MI 48909.

This free handbook was developed for use by public libraries. It gives an overview of libraries and literacy and includes tips on developing a collection for adult new readers.

Lyman, Helen Huguenor. **Literacy and the Nation's Libraries.**
Chicago: American Library Association, 1977.
211p. Bibliography. Glossary. Index. ISBN 0–08389–0244–8.

This manual was developed as a collaborative effort by the American Library Association and librarians, educators, publishers, and others throughout the United States. It is intended to guide libraries in developing workable, effective ways to help "people of all ages and all reading levels to become competent, habitual and independent readers." The collaborators seek to avoid repetition of work already being done by others, and to increase cooperation and the planning and implementation of joint programs, in part by helping librarians evaluate existing programs.

_____. **Reading and the Adult New Reader.**
Chicago: American Library Association, 1976.
ISBN 0–8389–0228–6.

Although now out of print, this book has been considered a standard resource, particularly for librarians interested in meeting the special needs of adult new readers. It discusses the reading process and explains how to evaluate and select materials for adult new readers, with an emphasis on the ways attitudes, beliefs, and values influence readers.

Mayer, Steven E. **Guidelines for Effective Adult Literacy Programs.**
Minneapolis, MN: B. Dalton Bookseller National Literacy Initiative, 1984.
Bibliography. Looseleaf. Available through the following organizations: Association for Community Based Education, 1806 Vernon Street, NW, Washington, DC 20009; Council of State Directors of Adult Education, Room 229, State House, Indianapolis, IN 46204; Laubach Literacy Action, P.O. Box 131, Syracuse, NY 13210; or Literacy Volunteers of America, 5795 Widewaters Parkway, Syracuse, NY 13214.

Guidelines was developed under the auspices of the B. Dalton Bookseller National Literacy Initiative. It was intended to provide guidance by describing the ingredients that make up a successful adult literacy program rather than by listing step-by-step instructions. The guidelines stress the primary concern of literacy programs—supporting adult learners in attaining literacy skills—rather than program management. The looseleaf guide is divided into seven chapters, each of which focuses on a key component of a literacy program: Community, Adult Learners, Staff Resources, Instruction and Support, Governance, Management, and Evaluation. Each chapter includes a program assessment checklist of items related to the guidelines discussed in the chapters. Two appendixes are included: a list of suggested items for inclusion in program records and a resource bibliography.

Smith, Carl B., and Leo C. Fay. **Getting People To Read: Volunteer Programs That Work.**
New York: Delacorte Press, 1973.
238p. Bibliography. LC 73–7538.

This handbook, part of a National Book Committee project to increase reading experience and opportunity, consolidates information gleaned from intensive research of volunteer outreach reading programs around the country. Based on the premise that individual, lay volunteers can make valuable contributions to solving "this persistent social problem," it offers practical guidelines and advice to individuals and organizations interested in setting up or improving volunteer literacy programs.

U.S. Conference of Mayors. **Adult Literacy: A Policy Statement and Resource Guide for Cities.**
Washington, DC: U.S. Conference of Mayors, 1986.
20p. Free. U.S. Conference of Mayors, 1620 Eye Street, NW, Washington, DC 20006.

This report is an expansion of a policy resolution, passed unanimously at the mayors' 1985 conference, that calls upon cities to join forces in developing coordinated literacy efforts and promoting local and national legislation that addresses the needs of illiterate adults. The resource guide contains specific guidelines for starting a mayoral literacy initiative, promoting public awareness, coordinating citywide efforts, and using resources such as libraries, churches, schools, the media, and unions for service delivery. It also contains a section on literacy program components and annotated lists of national resources and organizations involved in literacy research.

Yearbook

ALA Yearbook: A Review of Library Events.
Chicago, IL: American Library Association. 1976 – .

Each year, the American Library Association yearbook contains a section on literacy and libraries. In 1976, the entry was written by Jean Coleman; subsequent entries have been written by Helen Lyman. Each year's entry discusses events of the previous year involving libraries and literacy, including legislation; statistics; surveys and studies; local, state, and national programs; publications; article citations; and resources.

Monographs

Adult Performance Level (APL) Project. **Final Report: The Adult Performance Level Study.**
Austin, TX: APL Project, 1977.

This report gives a detailed breakdown and analysis of the Adult Performance Level (APL) study, which was sponsored by the U.S. Department of Education and carried out by a team at the University of Texas at Austin over several years in the early 1970s. The report presents the theory and methodology used in the study and breaks down the competencies of U.S. adults as measured by the survey in the areas of occupationally related knowledge, consumer economics, government and law, health, community resources, reading, writing, computation, and problem solving. Competency levels are also broken down by demographic groups. The report goes on to discuss the implications of the study for adult and elementary and secondary education. Four appendixes include a list of the APL objectives; a description of sample design and field procedures; a description of the scoring process used for the APL test items, and a report on the external competency-based high school diploma pilot program developed and carried out by the project staff.

Association for Community Based Education (ACBE). **Adult Literacy: Study of Community Based Literacy Programs.**
Washington, DC: ACBE, 1983, rev. 1986.
2 vols. $15.

In 1983, the Association for Community Based Education (ACBE) conducted an extensive study of community-based literacy programs around the United States. This revised edition of the study's report is in two volumes. The first, a narrative of the study, describes the principles that guide community-based literacy programs; the second profiles and describes 32 programs.

Bailey, Richard W., and Robin Melanie Fosheim, eds. **Literacy for Life: The Demand for Reading and Writing.**
New York: Modern Language Association of America, 1983.
272p. ISBN 0–87352–130–7; ISBN 0–87352–131–5 (paper).

Literacy for Life is a diverse collection of speculative essays examining literacy in the 1980s. Intended for teachers, educational policy makers, and "those ... who would influence the influential," the articles are grouped into four sections. The first explores literacy in social contexts;

the second explores the relationship of print literacy to the use of other media, including telecommunications; the third centers on literacy uses in a variety of professions and jobs; and the fourth focuses on classroom practices in the teaching of reading and writing.

Carroll, John B., and Jeanne S. Chall, eds. **Toward a Literate Society: Report of the Committee on Reading of the National Academy of Education, with a Series of Papers Commissioned by the Committee.**
New York: McGraw-Hill, 1975.
370p. Bib. references. Index. $24.95. ISBN 0–07–010130–2.

The Committee on Reading was formed in 1969 to provide guidance for Right to Read, an ambitious program with the goal (unmet) of achieving universal functional literacy in the United States by 1980. Part One of this book is the committee's report; Part Two is a collection of papers on topics ranging from the definition of reading literacy to the role of television in literacy programs to the political, economic, and financial implications of a national reading effort.

Childers, Thomas, and Joyce Post. **The Information-Poor in America.**
Metuchen, NJ: Scarecrow Press, 1975.
182p. Bibliography. Index. ISBN 0–8108–0775–0.

This is the final report of a study entitled Knowledge/Information Needs of the Disadvantaged, which was undertaken in 1972 under a grant from the Bureau of Libraries and Learning Resources under the U.S. Office of Education. The study consisted primarily of a literature review intended to provide directions for further research. The report examines literature related to the types of information sought and used by adults, the ways in which people obtain information, the quality and usefulness of that information, and how the ability—or inability—to locate and use information affects people's lives. It briefly examines the major groups of information-poor adults and identifies broad areas for future inquiry; for example, the effectiveness of communication through television and through increased interpersonal contact.

Cook, Wanda Dauksa. **Adult Literacy Education in the United States.**
Newark, DE: International Reading Association, 1977.
139p. Bibliography. ISBN 0–87207–934–1.

This succinct summary of efforts at adult literacy education from 1900 through the mid-1970s is useful for those seeking a deeper understanding of literacy education in a historical perspective. Each chapter covers a single decade, with sections on Social Climate, The Statistics, Legislation, Programs, Method and Materials, Professional Activities, and a Summary. Cook notes in her introduction that "the federal government's concern with the problem surfaces mainly during times of national conflict. The history is one which is characterized by individual efforts implemented by state and local governments. The reader's attention is focused primarily on the legislation, programs, and methods and materials which have resulted from these independent actions."

Copperman, Paul. **The Literacy Hoax: The Decline of Reading, Writing and Learning in the Public Schools and What We Can Do About It.**
New York: William Morrow, 1978.
323p. Bibliography. Index. $10.95; $5.95 paper. ISBN 0–688–03353–9; ISBN 0–688–08353–6 (paper).

The Literacy Hoax is a controversial, thought-provoking report by the owner/operator of a private reading school. Copperman attributes the decline in student achievement in the United States (which he documents) to an open education policy that declares learning should be entertaining and that gives children too much latitude in choosing what they will and will not learn. In the process, he maintains, students are allowed to complete school without acquiring essential skills.

Disch, Robert. **The Future of Literacy.**
Englewood Cliffs, NJ: Prentice-Hall, 1973.
177p. Bibliography. ISBN 0–13–346023–1.

In this provocative collection of essays, contributors such as Claude Levi-Strauss, Marshall McLuhan, Herbert Marcuse, Antonin Artaud, Eugene Ionesco, and others explore the implications and historical background of the statement, "The written word does not have long to live." Part One examines the impact of literacy historically and culturally. Part Two is divided into two sections: Literacy, Language, and Politics; and Literature under Attack. Part Three looks at The Future: Literacy and the Media. Among the ideas put forward are that mass phonetic literacy and a "glut of print" demean true (i.e., critical and imaginative) literacy and threaten its future; that the dominance of the printed word stifles thinking and discovery, leads to exploitation of people by those in power, and threatens oral culture; and that print, although it may survive for certain functional uses, may not remain viable as a medium for spiritual-aesthetic uses and literary culture.

Duggan, Paula. **Literacy at Work.**
Washington, DC: Northeast-Midwest Institute, 1985.
*24p. $5 plus $2 shipping. Publications Department, 218 D Street, SE,
Washington, DC 20003.*

This report examines the effects and consequences of illiteracy as it
relates to employment and the economy, particularly with respect to
displaced workers who need to upgrade basic skills in order to qualify for
new job training. It goes on to identify specific steps employers, schools,
public agencies, and state and federal government can take to improve
the situation. The report includes a number of examples of successful
programs at various levels.

Eberle, Anne, and Sandra Robinson. **The Adult Illiterate Speaks Out:
Personal Perspectives on Learning To Read and Write.**
Washington, DC: U.S. Department of Education, National Institute of
Education, 1980.
49p. Bibliography.

This poignant report draws from conversations and interviews with
illiterate and formerly illiterate adults to describe the experience of
being illiterate, deciding to become literate, and undergoing the process
of becoming literate. The report attempts to separate the mythologies of
illiteracy from its realities and to place illiteracy in a context of social,
economic, physical, and psychological factors. The authors also describe
how Vermont's Adult Basic Education (ABE) program, beginning in
1974, shifted its emphasis from part-time evening classes taught by
professional teachers in public school buildings to a year-round, in-
home tutoring program using volunteers. The shift resulted in a nearly
threefold increase in the number of adults served between 1974 and
1979, with little additional cost.

Fingeret, Arlene. **Adult Literacy Education: Current and Future
Directions.**
Columbus, OH: ERIC Clearinghouse on Adult, Career, and Vocational
Education, 1984.
56p. $5.50.

This is a thorough and thoughtful analysis of literacy-related literature
in the Educational Resources Information Center (ERIC) database,
including research reports; informal accounts; manuals and handbooks;
and theoretical, philosophical, and policy articles; plus references from
related fields and a sampling of books published between 1979 and 1984.
The report examines the literature base, underlying issues, program
models, program aspects, and the future of U.S. adult literacy education.
Fingeret ends with a call to literacy educators to make a commitment to

self-investigation of efforts, collaboration across program boundaries, and transcendence of disciplinary or organizational loyalties; she also cites a need for additional research and development efforts in the areas of reading, volunteerism, and competency-based education.

Freire, Paulo (trans. by Myra Bergman Ramos). **Pedagogy of the Oppressed.**
New York: Continuum Publishing, 1984 (22d printing, trans. from Portuguese in 1968).
186p. ISBN 0–8264–0047–7.

———— (trans. by Donaldo P. Macedo). **The Politics of Education: Culture, Power and Liberation.**
South Hadley, MA: Bergin & Garvey Publishers, 1985.
209p. Index. ISBN 0–89789–042–6; ISBN 0–89789–043–4 (paper).

Paulo Freire is known and respected worldwide for his work with illiterate adults in a number of Third World countries, particularly his native Brazil. His theories and philosophy of education and literacy and their relationship with political structure and people's lives, and in particular his work with community-based education, have significantly influenced literacy practice and theory in many countries, including the United States. In *Pedagogy of the Oppressed,* the first of his many books to be translated and published in this country, Freire expresses a radical concept of education as a tool for enabling all people to deal critically and effectively with the world in which they find themselves. The methods for such education should not be through "paternalistic" teacher-student relationships, which promote conformity and noncritical acceptance, but through a process of self-discovery and emancipation in which "[people] educate each other through the mediation of the world." *The Politics of Education* is a collection of brief essays written during the last few years in English and Spanish; it also includes the texts of two interviews with Dr. Freire.

Graff, Harvey J., ed. **Literacy and Social Development in the West: A Reader.**
Cambridge, England: Cambridge University Press, 1981.
340p. Bib. references. ISBN 0–521–23956–0; ISBN 0–521–28372–8 (paper).

This is a collection of scholarly essays, many of them selections from larger works, examining literacy and social development in Europe and North America from the eleventh century to the present. The editor has devoted his career to the study of literacy, particularly in a social and historical context. States Graff, "We are heirs to a body of thinking, a set of legacies about literacy and its imputedly vast import. A source of anxiety and confusion in a changing world, this is also a historical outcome that can only be understood in historical terms."

Harman, David. **Illiteracy, a National Dilemma.**
New York: Cambridge Book Company, 1987.
113p. Index. $11.95. ISBN 0–8428–2227–5.

In this brief but potent book, David Harman does much to debunk the myth of illiteracy as a social epidemic in search of a permanent cure, instead exploring its complex role in even more complex social, cultural, and economic settings. Harman tackles the difficult task of sorting out conflicting definitions of literacy and examines the limitations inherent in attempts to quantify literacy levels. He reviews the changing definitions and requirements for literacy from medieval times to the present and discusses the influence of cultural and social factors on the value of certain skills. Challenging the "national pastime" of blaming the schools for high illiteracy as well as a host of other problems, Harman points out that schools, after all, reflect their communities, and a community that does not value literacy will not support its schools in producing literate citizens. Essentially, literacy cannot be defined except within context, and an understanding of specific contexts is necessary for designing successful programs.

Hunter, Carman St. John, and David Harman. **Adult Illiteracy in the United States: A Report to the Ford Foundation.**
New York: McGraw-Hill, 1979, first paper ed. 1985.
208p. Annotated bibliography. Index. $8.95. ISBN 0–07–031369–5.

Adult Literacy in the United States was the culmination of a study funded by the Ford Foundation and carried out by World Education, Inc., in the late 1970s. It provides a comprehensive, contextual overview of adult illiteracy in the United States, including historical background, examination of statistical data, and evaluations of the various types of programs aimed at improving literacy skills, noting the enormous gap between publicly stated goals and actual achievements. The report concludes with a list of specific recommendations that call for a major shift in national educational policy and the establishment of community-based initiatives to serve the educational needs of disadvantaged adults. An updated summary of recommendations appears in the preface to the 1985 edition, with a warning that the problems of adult functional illiterates cannot be overcome by a single massive effort to teach everyone to read and write. The authors go on to propose a system of education "that serves the needs of citizens for access to appropriate education at whatever age and whatever level they require."

Kirsch, Irwin S., and Ann Jungeblut. **Literacy: Profiles of America's Young Adults.**
Princeton, NJ: Educational Testing Service, 1986.
68p. ISBN 0–88685–054–1. Center for the Assessment of Educational Progress at Educational Testing Service, Rosedale Road, Princeton, NJ 08541–0001.

This booklet summarizes the findings of a national study of young adults aged 21 to 25. For the study, the National Assessment of Educational Progress (NAEP) developed "literacy scales" that attempted to measure knowledge and skills in three areas: prose literacy, understanding and using information from texts that include editorials, news stories, poems, etc.; document literacy, locating and using information contained in documents such as job applications, bus schedules, and maps; and quantitative literacy, applying arithmetic operations that are embedded in printed materials, such as balancing a checkbook or figuring a tip. The study found that although 95 percent of those surveyed performed adequately at the lower levels of the three scales, many were unable to handle tasks of moderate complexity, and only a few were proficient at more complex and challenging tasks. The report concludes that the United States does not have an illiteracy problem—that is, that the vast majority of young adults have basic reading and writing skills—but that it does have a literacy problem, in that only a small percentage can understand and use complex material.

Kozol, Jonathan. **Illiterate America.**
Garden City, NY: Anchor Press/Doubleday, 1985.
270p. $15.95. ISBN 0–385–19536–2.

Jonathan Kozol's commitment to the spread of literacy and to the people whose cause he champions is unquestioned. This book, probably the most popularly known work on adult illiteracy, is more passionate than practical and more fiery than informative, perhaps purposely. Also, Kozol's carelessness with statistics damages the overall credibility of the book. *Illiterate America,* however, like Kozol himself, has gained considerable public notice, has been often quoted (though rarely questioned) and has served to focus attention on adult illiteracy as an issue.

Mezirow, Jack, Gordon G. Darkenwald, and Alan B. Knox. **The Last Gamble on Education.**
Washington, DC: Adult Education Association of the U.S.A., 1975.
206p. Bibliography. Index. $13, $11 for AAACE members. American Association for Adult and Continuing Education (AAACE), 1201 Sixteenth Street, NW, Suite 230, Washington, DC 20036.

This is an analytical study of urban Adult Basic Education (ABE) programs and practices, based on two national surveys and field work in six cities: New York; Boston; Detroit; San Francisco; San Jose, California; and Washington, DC. It focuses on program organization and functioning, classroom interaction, and the perspectives and characteristics of the individuals involved, particularly the students—their perceptions of the program, themselves, other students, and teachers; their motives for participating; what they hope to gain; and their perceived incentives and constraints. The roles, attitudes, and goals of teachers, paraprofessional aides, and program directors are also addressed.

National Advisory Committee on Adult Education. **Illiteracy in America: Extent, Causes, and Suggested Solutions.**
Washington, DC: U.S. Government Printing Office, 1986.
93p. Index. $4.75. Stock no. 065–000–00253–1. Superintendent of Documents, Department 36-UH, U.S. Government Printing Office, Washington, DC 20402–9325.

Illiteracy in America is a report commissioned to (1) determine reasons for widely varying statistics of illiteracy; (2) discuss why the public school system has not accomplished its task (i.e., transmitting literacy) to the satisfaction of many citizens; (3) recommend improvements, especially for the education system, to reduce and ultimately eradicate illiteracy. The report concentrates mainly on the second objective, distributing the blame for illiteracy among progressive education, drugs, television, permissive parents, and an excess of federal intervention. The lengthy list of recommendations tends to be idealistic and vague rather than practical and specific, for example: "Instill positive attitude and teach ethical behavior, especially in the early years." The report does not really address the issue of current adult illiteracy in the United States.

National Institute of Education. **APL Revisited: Its Uses and Adaptations in States.**
Washington, DC: U.S. Department of Education, 1980.
78p.

These two papers examining the Adult Performance Level (APL) study are aimed at adult educators involved in developing competency-based adult education programs. The first examines the competencies identified by APL in relation to 11 other efforts to identify skills necessary for adult life, two of which preceded APL. The author cautions that decisions made by study sponsors "will profoundly affect the substance of competency identification and the determination of which ones will be proposed as essential to success or survival." The paper includes a summary of competencies from the APL and other studies; these range from reading, writing, listening, and speaking to understanding advertising techniques and time zones. The second paper examines the role of the APL concept in adult basic education programs. The author questions the basic beliefs underlying the study, its definitions of success, and the way it was conducted, as well as whether it is possible to define a single set of knowledge and skills that constitute overall adult competence in our diverse society.

Northcutt, Norvell. **Adult Functional Competency: A Summary.**
Austin, TX: University of Texas at Austin, 1975.

This report summarizes the findings of the Adult Performance Level (APL) study, which undertook to identify and quantify skills and knowledge (called "competencies") required for economic and educational success in the contemporary United States. The list of competencies included knowledge of consumer economics, occupational information, community resources, health, government, and law, as well as basic reading, writing, and computational skills. Levels of mastery of functional competency were measured primarily by three criteria: education (number of years completed); occupational status, in which unskilled rated lowest and professional-managerial rated highest; and family income. The APL study has served as a basis for current Competency-Based Adult Education (CBAE) programs.

Pattison, Robert. **On Literacy: The Politics of the Word from Homer to the Age of Rock.**
New York: Oxford University Press, 1982.
246p. Bib. references. Index. $19.95; $6.95 paper. ISBN 0–19–503137–7; ISBN 0–19–503423–6 (paper).

In this extended essay, Pattison, a humanities instructor whose interest in literacy grew from his experiences teaching freshman English, offers a radical view of literacy and its function in societies from ancient times to the present: "American literacy is currently undergoing a fundamental redefinition of literacy. This redefinition is neither good nor bad, but mindless resistance to it in the name of preserving deliquescent concepts of language and unadapted technologies of language-use is almost certainly fatal to the preservation of culture."

Resnick, Daniel, ed. **Literacy in Historical Perspective.**
Washington, DC: Library of Congress, 1983.
ISBN 0–8444–0410–1. Superintendent of Documents, U.S. Government Printing Office, Washington, DC 20402.

This is a series of eight papers commissioned for a July 1980 conference cosponsored by the Library of Congress Center for the Book and the

National Institute of Education that brought together historians, educators, and government officials to discuss literacy research in progress and needed further research. Most interesting are the first three essays, which offer different perspectives on the development of literacy in medieval Europe and preindustrial England and New England. The essays contain some thought-provoking ideas on the relationship of literacy to economics, politics, religion, and social and cultural environments.

Skagen, Anne, ed. **Workplace Literacy.**
New York: American Management Association, 1986.
74p. $7.50 AMA members, $10 nonmembers, $3.75 students. ISBN 0–8144–2325–6.

This succinct report on the role of literacy in the workplace—and the role of the workplace in fostering literacy—was prepared as a management briefing for the American Management Association. The first chapter, by David Harman, explores definitions of workplace literacy in terms of real needs, as opposed to generic basic skills. The briefing then goes on to describe case studies of programs that have successfully linked basic, on-the-job skill requirements to educational programs; several successful corporate outreach programs; and major committees, coalitions, and nonprofit agencies dealing with illiteracy, such as the Business Council for Effective Literacy and Reading Is Fundamental.

Sticht, Thomas, William Armstrong, Daniel Hickey, and John Caylor. **Cast-off Youth: Policy and Training Methods from the Military Experience.**
New York: Praeger, 1987.

Although the armed forces have long been the country's largest employer and trainer of illiterate and low-literate youth, other government and private programs have had little knowledge of, and thus been unable to benefit from, the military's experience. *Cast-off Youth,* the result of two years of research, examines that experience in detail, with special emphasis on the Vietnam-era Project 100,000, a program intended to show that "cast-off youth," those with the lowest basic skills, could be trained for essential military jobs. The team found, among other things, that Project 100,000 participants were not only more successful in military life but have continued to earn more, have less unemployment, and be more likely to enroll in educational programs than nonparticipants. The report analyzes the implications of the research for civilian as well as future military practice, concluding that civilian programs could benefit from examination of the military's approach and from more research into how to develop curricula and methodology for teaching low-literate youth. Of particular interest is the success of a prototype electronics technician course that integrated basic skills training with a specialized field of knowledge, rather than attempting to impart basic skills outside of any specific context.

Thimmesch, Nick. **Aliteracy: People Who Can Read But Won't.**
Washington, DC: American Enterprise Institute for Public Policy Research, 1984.
60p. ISBN 0–8447–2247–2. American Enterprise Institute, 1150 17th Street, NW, Washington, DC 20036.

This is a collection of papers and discussions from a conference sponsored by the American Enterprise Institute for Public Policy Research. Topics include aliteracy as it relates to the newspaper and magazine industries, television and its effect on literacy, and the role of the schools in teaching reading. States American Enterprise Institute President William J. Baroody, Jr., "As difficult as the problems of the functionally illiterate may be, aliteracy may be the more dangerous problem because of its potential effects on the future of our nation. Aliteracy reflects a change in cultural values and a loss of skills, both of which threaten the processes of a free and democratic society."

Venezky, Richard L., Carl F. Kaestle, and Andrew M. Sum. **The Subtle Danger: Reflections on the Literacy Abilities of America's Young Adults.**
Princeton, NJ: Educational Testing Service, 1987.
61p. ISBN 0–88685–060–6. Report no. 16–CAEP–01.

This is a thoughtful and disturbing analysis of the 1984–1985 National Assessment of Educational Progress (NAEP) study of the literacy abilities of young adults, with particular emphasis on the study's findings as they relate to unemployment, economic competitiveness, poverty, and inequality among ethnic and socioeconomic groups. The authors summarize the results of the study and explore its implications not only as they relate to the labor market and education, but in terms of the mutual dependence of a democratic society and its citizens: "A democracy requires a well-informed citizenry for its survival and well-being, and every citizen within a society requires information for participation and advancement within that society."

Periodicals

Literacy education is an intensively active field, with constant changes in knowledge, ideas, attitudes, and activities; therefore periodicals constitute one of the best sources for current information. The following periodicals deal with illiteracy primarily from a national perspective; many state and local programs produce their own newsletters, which can provide valuable information about events closer to home.

Many of the periodicals listed do not claim copyright for all or part of each issue, in order to facilitate the spread of information. Check individual publications for explicit permission to reprint.

The AAACE Newsletter
American Association for Adult and Continuing Education (AAACE)
1201 Sixteenth Street, NW, Suite 230
Washington, DC 20036
(202) 822-7866
Monthly. Included with AAACE membership; nonmember subscription $20/year.

The American Association for Adult and Continuing Education (AAACE) is the country's largest professional association of adult educators. AAACE's newsletter features news on legislation and public policy, research, reports, statistics, conferences, trends, and innovative adult education programs. Issues also include profiles of adult educators and reviews of print and other resource materials.

Adult Education Clearinghouse Newsletter
Center for Continuing Education
Montclair State College
Upper Montclair, NJ 07043
Monthly. $14.50/year prepaid, $16 purchase order (payable to Center for Continuing Education).

This newsletter is a source of information on grants, recent publications, and upcoming events for Adult Basic Education, Adult Special Education, and English as a Second Language programs.

Adult Education Quarterly
American Association for Adult and Continuing Education (AAACE)
1201 Sixteenth Street, NW
Suite 230
Washington, DC 20036
(202) 822-7866
Quarterly. Included with AAACE membership; nonmember subscription $34/year ($41 for Canadian and foreign subscribers); or $65/year for package that includes Adult Education Quarterly *and* Lifelong Learning.

The American Association for Adult and Continuing Education (AAACE) publishes this research and theory journal, which features in-depth articles on research, methods, evaluation, and theory in the field of adult education.

Adult Literacy: Programs, Planning, Issues: A Newsletter for the Business Community
Business Council for Effective Literacy (BCEL)
1221 Avenue of the Americas
New York, NY 10020
(212) 512-2415/2412
Irregular. Free. Write or call to be placed on mailing list.

The Business Council for Effective Literacy (BCEL) was founded in 1984 to foster greater corporate awareness of adult functional illiteracy and to increase business involvement and support in the literacy field. The BCEL newsletter features current information on legislation and government, volunteer, and corporate programs around the country, plus book reviews and editorials by BCEL president and founder Harold W. McGraw, Jr. Most issues contain an in-depth article on an important aspect of adult illiteracy (sample titles: "The Broadcast Media and Literacy," "Libraries and Literacy," "The Case for Computers," "Behind Bars" (a look at programs in prisons). Back issues of the newsletter are available at no cost for up to six copies and $.25 per copy thereafter.

ALI Update: A Newsletter for the Adult Literacy Community
Adult Literacy Initiative (ALI)
Room 4145, FOB-6
400 Maryland Avenue, NW
Washington, DC 20202
(202) 732-2959
Quarterly. Free. Write or call to be placed on mailing list.

The Adult Literacy Initiative (ALI) was established at the U.S. Department of Education in 1983 to generate national awareness, promote public/private sector partnerships, provide technical assistance, and coordinate federal literacy programs. *ALI Update* contains a wide variety of current information on government (federal, state, and local) and privately administered literacy-related programs, research, funding allocations, grant programs, and other activities.

The CBE Report
Association for Community-Based Education (ACBE)
1806 Vernon Street, NW
Washington, DC 20009
(202) 462-6333
Biweekly. Included with ACBE membership; nonmember subscription $30/year.

The newsletter for the Association for Community-Based Education (ACBE) features association activities and workshops; national news; book reviews; resources, including computer systems; funding sources; and grant eligibility and application deadlines.

Focus on Basics
World Education
210 Lincoln Street
Boston, MA 02111
Three times/year. $10/year.

World Education is a nonprofit organization providing training and technical assistance in nonformal training for adults in the United States and around the world. *Focus on Basics* is a resource bulletin that provides information for adult educators on innovative and effective teaching practices used in basic skills programs around the United States. The emphasis is on approaches that involve learners in their own education and that assist teachers to develop low-cost, locally specific materials.

Instruction Delivery Systems
Communicative Technology Corporation
Attn: Magazine Subscription Department
50 Culpeper Street
Warrenton, VA 22186–3207
Bimonthly. $15/year; free to qualified professionals, including educators and trainers.

Instruction Delivery Systems is a magazine devoted to applications of technology to improve education, training, and job performance, with an emphasis on applications and issues related to learning technology. It includes news and in-depth coverage of technology-in-learning issues, plus commentary and insights by leaders in various fields, including business, industry, education, training, government, the military, and technological development. The first issue (January/February 1987) focused on "Technology vs. Illiteracy."

The Ladder
Push Literacy Action Now, Inc. (PLAN)
1332 G Street, SE
Washington, DC 20003
(202) 547-8903
Bimonthly. $10/year.

The Ladder is a national newsletter that provides information on legislation, funding, and other events affecting literacy education, as well as commentary and discussion on such topics as teaching and training alternatives, literacy activities outside the classroom, government action and inaction, and experiences and suggestions of students and teachers. Regular features include "Plain Talk," editorials on policy and politics; "State of the Art," articles by teachers and volunteers on literacy techniques; and "What If You Couldn't Read?" interviews with program participants.

Lifelong Learning: An Omnibus of Practice and Research
American Association for Adult and Continuing Education (AAACE)
1201 Sixteenth Street, NW
Suite 230
Washington, DC 20036
Eight times/year. Included with AAACE membership; nonmember subscription $35/year ($42 for Canadian and foreign subscribers); or $65/year for package that includes Lifelong Learning *and* Adult Education Quarterly.

Lifelong Learning is a professional journal for adult educators. It features a variety of practical and theoretical articles on innovative teaching strategies, instructional design, research, adult development, and trends and issues in professional adult and continuing education. Literacy and basic skills education are frequent topics. Regular features include book reviews and "Techniques," program ideas and tips for such areas as continuing and community education and professional development.

Literacy Advance
Laubach Literacy Action (LLA)
P.O. Box 131
Syracuse, NY 13210
(315) 422-9121
Quarterly.

Literacy Advance is the newsletter for Laubach Literacy Action (LLA), the U.S. program of Laubach Literacy International (LLI). In newspaper format, it covers national and local LLA activities, reviews of books and other materials, how-to's and tutoring tips, tutor-student success biographies, editorials, and general news related to literacy in the United States.

The Literacy Beat
National Education Writers Association (EWA)
1001 Connecticut Avenue, NW
Suite 310
Washington, DC 20036
(202) 429-9680

The Literacy Beat is the newsletter for the Media Resource Project on Literacy, a combined effort by National Education Writers Association (EWA, a professional organization of education reporters and editors) and the Institute for Educational Leadership. The purpose of the project is to increase awareness of literacy issues among the print and electronic media and to provide the media with resources for coverage of literacy issues. Activities include an information clearinghouse for editors and reporters, plus seminars, workshops, and a guidebook on covering literacy issues. *The Literacy Beat* focuses on specific aspects of literacy coverage such as definitions, intergenerational problems, workplace literacy, data sources and analyses, and civic literacy.

News for You
New Readers Press
P.O. Box 131
Syracuse, NY 13210
(800) 448-8878
(800) 624-6703 in New York
48 times/year. $.18/copy; 10 or more copies to the same address, $.15/copy; foreign subscriptions $.40/copy. Call for free sample copy.

News for You is a newspaper geared to the special reading needs of adult new readers. Written at a fourth- to sixth-grade reading level, it includes current national and international news stories; features; consumer, health and fitness, and legal rights information; and crossword puzzles. Each issue also includes a teacher's worksheet, "Focus," with prereading activities, vocabulary and scanning exercises, and discussion and opinion questions. Expanded issues, published once a month from October through May, feature in-depth coverage of selected topics; for example, leisure, weather, and photography.

The Reader
Literacy Volunteers of America (LVA)
5795 Widewaters Parkway
Syracuse, NY 13214
(315) 445-8000
Quarterly.

Literacy Volunteers of America (LVA) provides training, materials, technical assistance, and support to nonprofessional volunteer basic skills and English for Speakers of Other Languages (ESOL) tutors. LVA's newsletter features reports on LVA activities, legislation, tutor and student advice, and general national literacy news.

Reports Magazine
World Education
210 Lincoln Street
Boston, MA 02111
Semiannual. $15/year for organizations; $10/year for individuals.

Reports serves as a forum for discussing developments, sharing knowledge from innovative programs, and stimulating thinking on emerging issues in the field of adult education and training in the United States and abroad. Literacy is a frequent topic. *Reports* devoted its Spring 1987 issue to literacy, with a special focus on learners; that issue included articles by Carman St. John Hunter ("Literacy/illiteracy in an International Perspective") and David Harman ("Learning in the Workplace"). *Reports* plans to devote one issue each in 1988 and 1989 to literacy as International Literacy Year (1990) approaches.

Students Speaking Out
Laubach Literacy Action (LLA)
P.O. Box 131
Syracuse, NY 13210
Irregular.

Students Speaking Out is a newsletter written for and by new readers. The issues are printed on white paper for reproduction and distribution by literacy councils, Laubach Literacy Action (LLA) and Literacy Volunteers of America (LVA) affiliates, adult education programs, and other groups. The newsletter features student profiles, opinions, letters, poetry and art, information on student support groups, tips for tutors, and news of literacy events.

the written word
Contact Literacy Center
P.O. Box 81826
Lincoln, NE 68501
(402) 464-0602
Monthly. $10/year.

Contact Literacy Center is the national information clearinghouse for the Coalition for Literacy. *the written word* features a variety of literacy news and resource information. Topics include legislation; grant announcements; new books and other resource materials; business, corporate, and organizational literacy programs and initiatives; and featured local programs from around the country; plus updates on the center's toll-free national hotline.

6

Computer Network, Databases, and Nonprint Media

THIS CHAPTER LISTS NONPRINT SOURCES of information on literacy/illiteracy, including a computer communications network and online and computer-accessible databases. It also lists audio and video tapes, films, and television series dealing with the topic of literacy/illiteracy.

Computer Network

LitLine
SpecialNet
2021 K Street, NW
Suite 315
Washington, DC 20006
(202) 296-1800
$25 one-time setup charge, $15 minimum connect charges per month.

LitLine, a component of the national Adult Literacy Initiative and the Mayor's Commission on Literacy in Philadelphia, is a 24-hour national, computer-based communications network designed to provide current information and instant communication for persons concerned with adult literacy. LitLine services include electronic bulletin boards, electronic mail, and computer conferencing. Information available through bulletin boards includes news on funding; legislative and policy initiatives; federal, state, and local activities; volunteer, business, and industry efforts; innovative technology and media projects; services to special populations; research and development activities; and promising programs and practices. Hourly connect costs for LitLine range from $4 to $32, depending on the cost option selected, whether the connection is via a local access or a Telenet number, and the time of day. Training and support materials are available.

Databases

Online Databases

Education Index
Type:	Reference (bibliographic)
Producer:	H. W. Wilson Company 950 University Avenue Bronx, NY 10452
Updated:	Twice/week; about 3,000 records/month
Online Service:	WILSONLINE

Education Index contains approximately 50,000 citations to articles; interviews; editorials and letters to the editor; and reviews of books, educational films, and software from about 350 English-language periodicals, monographs, and yearbooks in the educational field, dating from September 1983. Among the areas covered are adult education, teacher and vocational education, and teaching methodology, plus a variety of curriculum areas.

Educational Resources Information Center (ERIC)
Type:	Reference (bibliographic)
Producer:	U.S. Department of Education Office of Educational Research and Development
Updated:	Monthly
Online Services:	BRS, BRS After Dark, BRS/BRKTHRU, BRS/Saunders Colleague, DIALOG Information Services, Knowledge Index, ORBIT Information Technologies Corporation, TECHDATA

The Educational Resources Information Center (ERIC) maintains a database of citations, with abstracts, to journal and report literature in education and education-related areas. Journal literature, which dates from 1969, corresponds to the *Current Index to Journals in Education (CIJE)*; report literature, which covers significant research and funded projects, corresponds to *Resources in Education (RIE)* and dates from 1966. Relevant areas include adult and vocational education, adult literacy/illiteracy, reading and communications skills, and urban education. About 1,400 *CIJE* and 1,200 *RIE* records are added to the database each month.

Grants and Contracts Weekly

Producer: Capitol Publications, Inc.

Updated: Weekly

Online
Service: NewsNet

Grants and Contracts Weekly covers nondefense federal grants and contracts, in areas such as education, training, research, and social services, that are available for companies, school districts, nonprofit institutions, and private firms. The database, which corresponds to *Federal Grants and Contracts Weekly,* typically includes news items; RFP and Grant Alerts; descriptions of federal procurement offers with contact name, telephone number, and due date (where available); descriptions of available grants with contract information, funds available, and funding history; and Grants Profiles, which consist of more detailed descriptions and analyses of specific federal grant programs.

Computer-Readable Databases (Not Online)

Data Users Services Division
U.S. Bureau of the Census
Washington, DC 20233
(301) 763-5820

In late 1987, the Census Bureau made available the computer-readable file containing the data gathered through a survey for the English Language Proficiency Study. The survey was done under contract to the Department of Education in 1982 and included approximately 15,000 persons, most of them children. Its primary purpose was to determine the number of English-deficient children living in non–English-speaking homes. The adult test used in the survey, an adaptation of the Measure of Adult English Proficiency (MAEP) test, was also administered to a control group of native-born adults. Data from the entire adult group were used by the Department of Education in 1986 to arrive at a model for estimates of adult illiteracy using standard census data. The tape available from the Census Bureau contains only the responses from the survey; it does not contain the study results found by the Department of Education.

National Center for Education Statistics (NCES)
U.S. Department of Education
400 Maryland Avenue, SW
Washington, DC 20202
(301) 436-7882

The National Center for Education Statistics collects, reports, and analyzes statistics on the condition of education in the United States, as well as conducting surveys in various areas of education. The center also designs data records systems, maintains databases, provides computer access to data, and disseminates data, analyses, publications, and tabulations in a variety of formats. Sources of information include reports, surveys, computer tapes, field consultation, published literature, and relevant commercial and government online databases. The NCES Data Systems Branch disseminates survey data tapes and selected non-Center files; purchase of tapes includes all necessary documentation, including file layouts, narratives, and survey forms. Among the available tapes are surveys and studies in the areas of adult and vocational education, teacher language skills, and high school dropouts.

Nonprint Media

Videocassettes and Films

The following include documentary and informational films and videos; training is not addressed. A number of films and videos are available on literacy instruction; a good source for information about these is the *Literacy Video Resource Guide* produced by Project Literacy U.S. (PLUS). Copies of the guide are available for $5.75 each from PLUS National Outreach, WQED, 4802 Fifth Avenue, Pittsburgh, PA 15213.

Adult Literacy
Type: Videocassette
Length: 12 min.
Producer: Education Commission of the States
Cost: Rental $15; purchase $30

Distributor: Education Commission of the States
1860 Lincoln Street
Suite 300
Denver, CO 80295
(303) 830-3692

This 12-minute video is intended for governors, legislators, and other state policy makers. It emphasizes the economic consequences of illiteracy.

Can't Read Can't Write

Type: Videocassette

Length: 60 min.

Producer: Capital Cities

Cost: Rental (UFC #90412) $20; purchase (#S00016) $139 for VHS or BETA (additional copies, $89 each), $167 for ¾" U-Matic (additional copies $107 each)

Distributor: University of Illinois Film Center
1325 South Oak St.
Champaign, IL 61820
(800) FOR-FILM
(800) 252-1357 in Illinois

This documentary uses interviews to profile the experiences of adults who have overcome illiteracy in a variety of places from Louisiana sugar plantations to industrial northeastern cities. It also focuses on some of the key national organizations involved in literacy education. Hosted by Johnny Cash, who starred as an illiterate in the 1981 TV movie "The Pride of Jesse Hallam," the documentary also includes interviews with educational experts and conversations with then–Secretary of Education Terrel Bell, literacy spokesperson Barbara Bush, and Anthony Alvarado, chancellor of the New York Board of Education.

The Prison Literacy Project

Type: Videocassette; ½" VHS format

Length: 27 min.

Cost: Purchase $75

Distributor: Prison Literacy Project
454 Maple Avenue
Jenkintown, PA 19406

Date: 1987

This video documentary covers the work and impact of the literacy program at the State Correctional Institution in Graterford, Pennsylvania.

Stories

Type:	Videocassette
Length:	18 min.
Cost:	$150 for VHS or BETA, $200 for U-Matic
Distributor:	Adair and Armstrong 900 Twenty-third Street San Francisco, CA 94107 (415) 826-6500
Date:	1984

Stories is part one of a four-part series, *Teaching Adults To Read,* that was created as a part of Project Read, the adult literacy program of the San Francisco Public Library and the Friends of the San Francisco Public Library. In *Stories,* five Project Read participants talk about how they feel about being nonreaders, how they cope with illiteracy, why they decided to seek help, and their hopes for the future. The video is divided into three sections, "Getting By" and "Early Years," in which students describe survival strategies, experiences, and concealment, and "Tutors and Students," which focuses on the interaction between tutor and student and student achievements. Compelling viewing, *Stories* could serve as a vehicle for such efforts as raising community awareness, recruiting students and volunteers, and fund raising.

What If You Couldn't Read?

Type:	16mm color film; videocassette
Length:	28 min.
Producer:	Dorothy Tod Films
Cost:	Rental $50; purchase $400 (film), $350 (videocassette)
Distributor:	Dorothy Tod Films 20 Bailey Avenue Montpelier, VT 05602
Date:	1978

What If You Couldn't Read? is the multiple-award-winning story of Vermont farmer Lyle Litchfield, who began learning to read in middle age with the help of an Adult Basic Education tutor. The film explores the strategies Lyle used to avoid being discovered, his success as a fur trader, and his changing relationship with his wife, Doris, as he attains literacy and independence. This film is unusual in its depiction of the effects—not always positive—of changes in literacy skills on families and friendships.

Audio Cassettes

Adult Illiteracy

Type: Cassette tape

Length: 60 min.

Producer: National Public Radio

Cost: $10.95 (order #OE-79-01-15)

Distributor: National Public Radio Customer Service
P.O. Box 55417
Madison, WI 53705
(800) 253-0808

In this radio documentary, instructors, authors, and illiterate adults discuss current teaching methods and problems of illiteracy.

Analfabetissmo: Illiteracy and Latinos

Type: Cassette tape

Length: 30 min.

Producer: Audrey Coleman, Readers' Radio

Cost: $10.95 (California add 6 percent sales tax) plus $2 postage and handling

Distributor Readers' Radio
P.O. Box 5053
Culver City, CA 90230

This documentary explores Hispanic literacy problems through interviews with students, educators, policy makers, and concerned parents, plus visits to programs that reflect the national Hispanic experience.

Is Civic Literacy at Risk?

Type: Cassette tape

Length: 60 min.

Producer: Sunrise Radio

Cost: $12.50

Distributor: Sunrise Radio
3110 South Wadsworth Boulevard, #304
Denver, CO 80227

This is a recording of a panel discussion (actually a series of speeches) held at the 1987 annual conference of the Education Commission of the States in Denver, Colorado, on the need for literacy in maintaining a democratic society. The speakers represent a range of opinions and approaches. Overall, the talks are intelligent, lively, and thought-provoking.

Perspectives on the Literacy Crisis in America

Type:　　　Cassette tape

Length:　　Three documentaries, 30 min. each; five report modules, 6 min. each

Producer:　Audrey Coleman, Readers' Radio

Cost:　　　$24.95 (California add 6 percent sales tax) plus $2 postage and handling

Distributor:　Readers' Radio
P.O. Box 5053
Culver City, CA 90230

The first documentary, "What Went Wrong?," explores the causes and costs of illiteracy through interviews with illiterates and educators. The second, "Another Chance," discusses alternatives available to adults who want to become literate, including night school classes, community centers, libraries, churches, and factories, and talks about the role of volunteers. The third, "The Politics of Literacy," investigates the responsibilities of federal, state, and local government, private business, and communities in combatting illiteracy. The modules consist of six-minute reports on each of five literacy efforts around the country—in Kentucky, Chicago, California, New York, and Washington, DC.

Understanding the Literacy Crisis: Ten Reports

Type:　　　Cassette tape

Length:　　Ten reports, 6 min. each

Producer:　Audrey Coleman, Readers' Radio, for Project Literacy U.S. (PLUS)

Cost:　　　$12.95 (California add 6 percent sales tax) plus $2 postage and handling

Distributor:　Readers' Radio
P.O. Box 5053
Culver City, CA 90230

This series of ten six-minute reports includes visits to programs, interviews with students, teachers, volunteers, and national literacy experts. The reports are titled "Functional Illiteracy: Combatting the Stereotypes"; "The Black Community: Assault on Illiteracy Program"; "Immigrant Literacy Students"; "Rural Women: Green County, Kentucky"; "The Role of Literacy Volunteers"; "Becoming Literate: Benefits and Costs of Change"; "Reading Disabilities: Are They Always Real?"; "The Influence of Paulo Freire: American Reading Council"; "Business and Literacy: People at Polaroid"; "Literacy as Ministry: The Role of Churches."

Television Series

American Ticket

Series: 30- and 15-min. programs, on videocassette, with supplemental viewer and instructor materials

Producer and distributor: KCET
4401 Sunset Boulevard
Los Angeles, CA 90027
(213) 667-9497

"American Ticket" was developed by Los Angeles public television station KCET as part of Project Literacy U.S. It is a series of 30- and 15-minute programs for broadcast on local public television stations. The programs, which take place on the job in a sign factory, emphasize literacy skills as they relate to employment. Objectives include enabling viewers to understand the basic principles of keeping a job and getting a promotion, performing simple arithmetic computations related to life skill situations, and recognizing job-related vocabulary terms. The series also seeks to help viewers develop positive outlooks regarding the benefits to be derived from adult education and to encourage them to get involved in local literacy or adult education programs and to stay in the programs once enrolled.

Humor is an important element in the programs, which also include "Success Stories," "Celebrity Pitches" by sports, business, and movie personalities, and at-home vignettes of series characters sharing reading and word activities with their children. The programs are supplemented by weekly viewer "video magazines," with activities and word-and-picture stories, and an instructor's guide for local literacy providers.

Another Page

Series: Fifteen programs, including an orientation program for teachers and students, plus three companion student books

Producer and distributor: KET Enterprise
2230 Richmond Road
Suite 213
Lexington, KY 40502
(800) 354-9067
(606) 233-3000 in Kentucky

GED on TV

Series: Forty-three 30-min. programs, plus student workbooks, student math formula booklet, teacher's guide, and computer supplement

Producer and distributor: KET Enterprise

Learn To Read

Series: Thirty 30-min. programs, plus a documentary on adult illiteracy

Producer: WXYZ-TV, Detroit

Distributor: KET Enterprise

Kentucky Educational Television produces a variety of educational video series for broadcast on public television stations and use by organizations. "Learn To Read" is aimed at beginning-level readers and emphasizes decoding skills, vocabulary building, and the advantages of learning to read. "Another Page," which is designed for adults who currently read between fifth- and eighth-grade levels as measured by the Fry formula, stresses reading and adult survival skills. The tapes in this series are grouped into three types of reading material: practical, including forms, leases, recipes, and reference books; general, including newspaper and magazine articles; and prose literature, including contemporary fiction, biography, and essays. "GED on TV," which was revised by KET in 1986, is designed to help adults develop the reading comprehension, writing, and mathematics skills needed to earn a high school equivalency certificate. The GED (General Educational Development) series includes computer disks for reinforcing learning with drills and practice exercises. Free review programs are available for each series.

Glossary

Adult Basic Education (ABE) (as defined by the Adult Education Act of 1966)   Education for persons whose inability to speak, read, or write the English language substantially impairs their ability to get or retain employment commensurate with their real abilities. Adult Basic Education is intended to raise the educational level of such persons in order to decrease their dependence on others, enable them to benefit from occupational training, increase their opportunities for more productive and profitable employment, and make them better able to meet their adult responsibilities.

adult education   Instruction designed to meet the needs of adults past the age of compulsory school attendance who have either completed or interrupted their formal education and who have primary occupations other than being full-time students; alternatively, instruction and services for adults who (1) lack the basic educational skills needed to function effectively in society, (2) have not earned a high school diploma or General Education Development (GED) certificate, and (3) are not required to be enrolled in school.

adult learning   Any experience through which an adult achieves a change in knowledge, skills, and/or attitudes; also, the acquiring by an adult of knowledge, skills, and/or attitudes. Adult learning does not necessarily involve formal instruction.

Adult Performance Level (APL) study   A five-year (1971–1975) study, sponsored by the U.S. Office of Education, that attempted to identify competencies required for economic and educational success, and then evaluated the extent to which those competencies are found in

147

the adult population in the United States. The APL study served as a basis for the development of curricula currently used in competency-based adult education programs. The study still serves as a basis for many current literacy statistics.

andragogy   The art and science of helping adults learn through an approach that takes into account the learning styles, needs, and attitudes of adult learners. *See also* pedagogy.

assessment   A process for determining the quantitative and/or qualitative value or worth of something; for example, of a specific need or skill.

basic skills   Fundamental competencies deemed necessary for achievement of academic success in speaking, listening, reading, writing, and mathematics. The successful acquisition of basic skills requires an integration of literacy, numerical, social, and problem-solving skills that prepare individuals to meet the changing demands of their social, economic, and work environments.

community-based organization   An organization that is representative of a particular community and that is controlled by members of the community it serves. Community-based organizations are typically involved in various activities such as employment development, community education, community organization, resource development, and outreach. Alternatively, a private nonprofit organization that is representative of a particular community and that provides employment and training services or activities.

competency   A demonstrated ability to succeed in a life-role activity, including having the generic knowledge and skill needed to perform effectively in a job or in a specific life role.

competency-based education (CBE)   A performance-oriented, individually paced process intended to lead to demonstrated mastery of basic and life skills needed to function effectively in society. Also referred to as competency-based adult education (CBAE).

coping skills   Skills that enable an individual to handle personal, social, and work-related problems and difficulties.

delivery system   An organizational and administrative arrangement for providing specific services, e.g., learning opportunities.

demand population   Persons who actually enroll in a program. The demand population for literacy programs in the United States is estimated at two to four million. *See also* target population.

disadvantaged adult   A person 16 years old or older who, due to physical, social, economic, educational and/or cultural limitations or barriers, is unable to participate fully in life's activities.

educationally disadvantaged adult   A person 16 years old or older who is not enrolled in school and who has not completed secondary school.

English as a Second Language (ESL); English for Speakers of Other Languages (ESOL)   A program designed to enable persons whose native language is other than English to study and develop English-language skills, including speaking, listening, reading, and writing.

external high school diploma program   An evaluation system through which adults can earn high school diplomas by demonstrating generalized competency in life skills and specific competency in entry-level occupational skills, advanced academic work, or a special ability in an area such as art or music.

formal education   An organized set of educational activities that, when successfully completed, entitle an individual to a degree, diploma, license, or other official document. *See also* nonformal education.

functional competency   The ability to perform practical everyday activities through application of basic skills.

General Educational Development (GED) Program   A program of instruction designed to prepare persons to take a high school equivalency examination.

high school equivalency examination   An examination or set of examinations intended to determine a learner's achievement or performance in the general subject areas normally required for graduation from high school. Upon passing the tests, an individual is awarded a certificate that is considered equivalent to a high school diploma. The most widely recognized such examinations are the Tests of General Educational Development (GED).

mid-level literacy   The possession of basic reading, writing, and computation skills (i.e., fifth- to ninth-grade level) but not of higher-level critical thinking skills.

nonformal education   Organized educational activity that takes place outside the established formal education system and for which learners do not receive official recognition on completion. Nonformal education may operate independently or be a feature of some broader activity intended to serve specific clienteles and learning objectives. *See also* formal education.

pedagogy   The art, practice, or profession of teaching. *See also* andragogy.

target population   Persons who are or could be considered candidates for a particular program.

Tests of General Educational Development (GED)   A set of academic achievement tests designed to measure whether a person possesses the knowledge, skills, and understanding usually acquired through a high school education. Most state departments of education issue certificates of high school equivalency to individuals who successfully complete the tests.

tutoring   Instruction conducted on an individual basis, usually by a private teacher or instructor.

References

Adams, Frank. *Unearthing Seeds of Fire: The Idea of Highlander.* Winston-Salem, N.C. J. F. Blair, 1975.

Adult Performance Level (APL) Project. *Final Report: The Adult Performance Level Study.* Austin, TX: APL Project, 1978.

Cook, Wanda Dauksa. *Adult Literacy Education in the United States.* Newark, DE: International Reading Association, 1977.

Education Commission for the States (ECS). *Action for Excellence: A Comprehensive Plan To Improve Our Nation's Schools.* Denver, CO: ECS, 1983.

Guthrie, John T., and Mary Seifert. "Profiles of Reading in a Community," *Journal of Reading* 29 (March 1983): 498–508.

Harman, David. *Illiteracy: A National Dilemma.* New York: Cambridge Book Company, 1987.

Hunter, Carman St. John, and David Harman. *Adult Illiteracy in the United States: A Report to the Ford Foundation.* New York: McGraw-Hill, 1979 and 1985.

Irwin, Paul M. *Adult Literacy Issues, Programs, and Options.* Washington, DC: Congressional Research Service, 1986.

Isenberg, Irwin, ed. *The Drive Against Illiteracy.* New York: H. W. Wilson Company, 1964.

Kirsch, Irwin S., and Ann Jungeblut. *Literacy: Profiles of America's Young Adults.* Princeton, NJ: Educational Testing Service, 1986.

Lerche, Renee. *Effective Adult Literacy Programs: A Practitioner's Guide.* New York: Cambridge Book Company, 1985.

Lockridge, Kenneth A. *Literacy in Colonial New England: An Enquiry into the Social Context of Literacy in the Early Modern West*. New York: W. W. Norton, 1974.

Ohles, John F., ed. *Biographical Dictionary of American Educators*. Westport, CT: Greenwood, 1978.

National Advisory Council for Adult Education (NACAE). *A History of the Adult Education Act*. Washington, DC: NACAE, 1980.

————. *Illiteracy in America: Extent, Causes, and Suggested Solutions*. Washington, DC: U.S. Government Printing Office, 1986.

National Institute for Education. *APL Revisited: Its Uses and Adaptations in States*. Washington, DC: U.S. Department of Education, 1980.

Northcutt, Norvell. *Adult Functional Competency: A Summary*. Austin, TX: Adult Performance Level (APL) Project, 1975.

Putnam, John F. *Adult Learning Activities Terminology*. Washington, DC: National Center for Education Statistics, 1982.

Sharon, Amiel T. "What Do Adults Read?" *Reading Research Quarterly* 9, no. 2 (1973–1974): 148–169.

Soltow, Lee, and Edward Stevens, *The Rise of Literacy and the Common School in the United States: A Socioeconomic Analysis to 1870*. Chicago: University of Chicago Press, 1982.

U.S. Bureau of the Census. *English Language Proficiency Study: MAEP Written Test: Adult*. Washington, DC: U.S. Bureau of the Census, 1982.

Venezky, Richard L., Carl F. Kaestle, and Andrew M. Sum. *The Subtle Danger: Reflections on the Literacy Abilities of America's Young Adults*. Princeton, NJ: Educational Testing Service, 1987.

Index

153

McCreary, James, 6
McDonald, Barbara J., 113
McGraw, Harold W., Jr., 36–37, 97
McGuffey's readers, 4
McNamara, Margaret, 107
MAEP. *See* Measure of Adult English Proficiency
Managing Money (Shelton), 39
Manpower Development and Training Act (MDTA), 14
MAR. *See* Montana All-purpose Readability index
Massachusetts, 3–6, 109
Materials and Methods in Adult and Continuing Education (Shelton), 39
Mayer, Steven E., 117
Mayor's Commission on Literacy of Philadelphia, 86
MDTA. *See* Manpower Development and Training Act
Measure of Adult English Proficiency (MAEP), 52–53
Measuring literacy, 48–50
Media Resource Guide, 102
Meeting the Challenge: Creative Reading Instruction in the Classroom (Askov), 24
Men, reading habits, 71
Mezirow, Jack, 125
Michigan, 6, 116
Military, 3, 6, 10–11, 17
Minneapolis Foundation, 108
Minnesota, 5–6, 20
Mississippi, 5–7
Modern Practice of Adult Education: From Pedagogy to Andragogy (Knowles), 32, 115
Montana All-purpose Readability (MAR) index, 75
Moonlight schools, 5–6

Moonlight Schools for the Emancipation of Adults (Stewart), 41
Mother's First Book (Stewart), 41

NAEF. *See* National Adult Education Foundation
NAEP. *See* National Assessment of Educational Progress
National Adult Education Foundation (NAEF), 94
National Adult Literacy Congress, 22
1987 proclamations, 86–89
National Adult Literacy Project, 19
National Advertising Council, 93
National Advisory Committee on Adult Education, 126
National Advisory Committee on Education, 9
National Adivsory Council on Adult Education, 76, 105
National Assessment of Educational Progress (NAEP), 20
adult reading habits survey, 68–73
Young Adult Study, 58–65
National Association for Public Continuing Adult Education, 94
National Association for Public School Adult Education, 13
National Center for Education Statistics (NCES), 140
National Commission for Adult Literacy, 12
National Conference of Mayors, 91
National Conference on Adult Education and the Negro, 10

Designed by Tanya Nigh
Composed in Helvetica and Century Schoolbook
Typeset by The TypeStudio, Santa Barbara, California
Printed and bound by Braun-Brumfield, Ann Arbor, Michigan